FAITH, THE **CHURCH,** AND THE **REAL** **WORLD**

A REDEMPTORIST PASTORAL PUBLICATION

Introduction by Mary Beth Yount, PhD

Liguori

CONTENTS

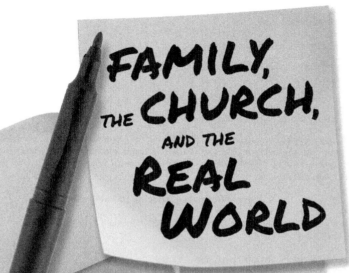

FAMILY, the CHURCH, and the REAL WORLD

Imprimi Potest:
Stephen T. Rehrauer, CSsR, Provincial
Denver Province, the Redemptorists

Published by Liguori Publications
Liguori, Missouri 63057

To order, visit Liguori.org or call 800-325-9521.

Library of Congress Cataloging-in-Publication Data

Family, the church, and the real world / introduction by Mary Beth Yount, PhD.
    pages cm
  ISBN 978-0-7648-2620-7
1. Families—Religious aspects—Catholic Church.
2. Marriage—Religious aspects—Catholic Church. 3. Church.
4. Catholic Church—Doctrines. I. Liguori Publications.
  BX2351.F3548 2015
  261.8'358—dc23
                          2015020620
p ISBN 978-0-7648-2620-7
e ISBN 978-0-7648-7053-8

Liguori Publications, a nonprofit corporation, is an apostolate of the Redemptorists. To learn more about the Redemptorists, visit Redemptorists.com.

Printed in the United States of America
19 18 17 16 15 / 5 4 3 2 1
First Edition

The Real World

INTRODUCTION

I know you don't have a lot of time to read. You have children to take care of, a house to clean, and more work to do than you can stand to think about. (Sorry for reminding you.) I'm with you on this. I have four children and a much-too-long list of tasks that I am successfully ignoring right now. But making time for this book is worth the investment because you will be inspired by a unique blend of Church teaching with practical advice, tips, and activities. The fruits of reading this book will extend to your family, your neighborhood, your parish, and our larger Church and world. The practical ideas in each chapter build on the presentation of Church teaching so that you not only understand Catholic teaching better but can immediately begin putting this deeper understanding into action.

Let me illustrate the need for this book with a story. One morning when I was a young theology professor, standing in front of my class explaining the Church's teaching on marriage and sexuality, an undergraduate student piped up: "I think the Catholic Church just needs to mind its own business!" "Yeah," exclaimed another, "Why does the Church think it can tell us what to do in our own bedrooms?" The floodgates opened. The students expressed that they felt as if the Church were trying to control their private actions and private lives. They were resentful, and a common theme was, "What right does the Church have to...?"

This was a turning point in my professional life. I suddenly realized that we, as a Church, do not convey often enough the gift bestowed on us by the Church's teaching about marriage. Instead, we focus on the nuances of moral teachings without situating them in the larger context. By not explaining the foundations of the Church's moral teaching, we miss the opportunity to help people discover that having a better relationship with God and one another can be an answer to the human restlessness we all feel. Because my students did not realize that Church teachings on marriage, the family, and sexuality are rooted in what it means to be human and our ultimate calling to love one another and God, they felt resentful of Church teaching. And this is not just the case with college students—I'm sure you hear similar comments at play dates, at work, in the media, even in church communities.

We all need more than just an understanding of what the Church teaches. We need support in how to allow this wisdom to fill us up and flow through our lives. A lot of people express that the Church is out of touch on issues related to family, sexuality, and the indissolubility of marriage. Why is it that so many people think our Catholic understanding of marriage is irrelevant to real life? Why do they express that Church teaching is something "out there," a bunch of impossible ethical standards to which people can never measure up?

That morning I began my search for answers to these questions, along with my mission of developing better ways to help people understand and live Church teaching. There is a lot for people to sort through around these issues. They hear things from the Church about the benefits of having a married mother and father, but they look around and see that this is not happening as often as it sounds like it should. In fact, a recent Pew study shows that in 2014 only 16 percent of households in the United States "included a married couple raising their own children" (compared to 1960, when almost 40 percent did).[1] Additionally, nine times more households with minor children in the U.S. are headed by a single father than in 1960.[2]

Add to these statistics families like mine, in which my husband and I are married and raising our own children with plenty of struggles and challenges. We enter into what people see as the "real": the imperfect. No wonder people feel confused. They hear all of these ideals from the Church, which aren't being perfectly lived out, and they begin to think there is a problem with the ideal. But the fact that none of us has a perfect family life is not a reproach. It is, in fact, just like the rest of life. None of us has perfect finances either, or perfect jobs, or a perfect government, or perfect anything. We are in the already but not

---

[1] Pewresearch.org/fact-tank/2014/04/30/5-facts-about-the-modern-american-family, accessed April 1, 2015.

[2] Pewsocialtrends.org/2013/07/02/the-rise-of-single-fathers, accessed April 1, 2015.

yet. We can continually grow, striving toward holiness and better relationships.

People are less emotional reading an article providing financial advice than they are when they hear teaching on the family. People feel differently about their less-than-ideal families and relationships than they do about their less-than-ideal finances because family life hits deeper emotions. The response of my students and similar responses from others are strong precisely because people care deeply about issues related to relationships. They care so intensely about families, marriages, and expressions of sexuality because they recognize that these hold profound meaning: that to be in loving relationships is part of who and what we were created to be. There is, in all of us, a deep sense that we are called to a loving relationship with one another and with God. These relationships can take different forms—such as married or single, religious, or lay—but we can all live them better.

Instead of making us feel burdened by shortcomings, learning about Church teaching and how to apply it to our lives can help bring us closer to the joy for which we were created. Every one of us can improve in our relationship with God and one another on our journey toward holiness. What a blessing to have this journey, this life, this capacity to love. And we are very blessed to have the Church's signposts along the way and a community of people who can share their tips for living this out more fully. We can all provide support and encouragement as we celebrate the joys and struggles together.

This book aims to give you, in an entertaining and conversational way, some background on Church teaching and then ideas for how to connect this to the individual family by providing actual steps so that you can immediately begin applying what you have read. Each author is an expert in his or her particular area of family life, and every chapter ends with suggestions for practical application. And the best news is that this book provides a community of support for all of us who are working to improve ourselves, our relationships, and our families. Join us: Read the *Family, the Church, and the Real World*.

DR. MARY BETH YOUNT

Director of Content and Programming,
World Meeting of Families (Philadelphia, 2015);
Professor of Theology, Neumann University

THE CHURCH

MASS

ADORATION @ 7:00PM

YOUTH GROUP MEETING

FAMILY, SCRIPTURE, AND THE SACRAMENTS:

HOLINESS THROUGH FAMILY LIFE IN THE SACRAMENT OF MARRIAGE

THOMAS J. NEAL, PHD

MARRIAGE AS MARTYRDOM

I remember vividly my wedding day back in 1995, on October 14. It was also the feast of Pope St. Callistus I, who was martyred in the year 222 during a time of fierce hostility toward Christians in the Roman Empire. To be openly Christian in those days was a risky choice to make! But imagine, without those many men and women who did take the risk and choose to publicly proclaim the Gospel, where would we be? We need more daring witnesses! In fact, I'd say the Church is always in need of new martyrs, and those who choose to give themselves to each other in holy wedlock—freely, exclusively, totally, faithfully, irrevocably, and fruitfully—are making their own kind of heroic act in this day and age!

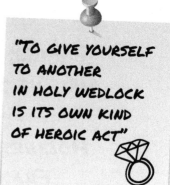

"TO GIVE YOURSELF TO ANOTHER IN HOLY WEDLOCK IS ITS OWN KIND OF HEROIC ACT"

Marriage as martyrdom might not sound very romantic but I'd say if you think about it, it's a supremely romantic image for marriage because the heart of a martyr is marked by selfless love in service to another. Wouldn't you feel afire with romantic love if you knew your spouse was willing daily to lay down a whole lifetime for you? It's no mistake that Valentine's Day is also the feast of a bloody martyrdom! Deep down, we're made for giving and receiving selfless love.

One of my wife's dear friends, who was himself long-married at the time, took me aside only minutes before our wedding began and said to me: "Tom, people will tell you that marriage brings you happiness, completes you, makes you whole. But here's the real truth—in the final analysis you get married for really only one reason: to become saints and to make saints of your kids. And like martyrdom, it ain't pretty." I recall thinking this poor man must've been jaded by life somehow or was blinded by some bitterness toward his wife. Why couldn't he see how wonderful and happy marriage could really be? Yet now, twenty years later, I view his wisdom much more clearly. His message was not that marriage and family life are unhappy things, but that real happiness is something different from what society calls happiness. Happiness—or better, joy—is the fruit of love, and real love costs. Marriage isn't about me, or even about us. It's about God and all the people God will one day ask us to welcome into the ambit of our marital love.

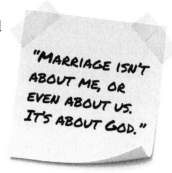

"MARRIAGE ISN'T ABOUT ME, OR EVEN ABOUT US. IT'S ABOUT GOD."

MARRIAGE AS LIFELONG UNION

Pope Francis captured the sacrificial and countercultural character of Christian marriage and family life beautifully at the 2013 World Youth Day in Brazil. He said:

> God calls you to make definitive choices, and he has a plan for each of you: to discover that plan and to respond to your vocation is to move forward toward personal fulfillment. God calls each of us to be holy, to live his life, but he has a particular path for each one of us. Some are called to holiness through family life in the sacrament of Marriage. Today, there are those who say that marriage is out of fashion....They say that it is not worth making a lifelong commitment, making a definitive decision, "forever," because we do not know what tomorrow will bring. I ask you, instead, to be revolutionaries, I ask you to swim against the tide; yes, I am asking you to rebel against this culture that sees everything as temporary and that ultimately believes you are incapable of responsibility, that believes you are incapable of true love.

Marriage is the vocation given to us by God at the dawn of human history, cleaving to one another in the covenant bond of love that is a fruitful, faithful, unbreakable, and total sharing of life. All of civilization rests on the strength of this bond, as this bond rests on the strength of God.

I love to think of every wedding day as a fresh re-presenting of God's original act of creating humanity as male and female in his image and likeness, calling the one man and the one woman to enter a face-to-face, one-flesh communion of love. God is truly the architect and archetype of human love! The one-flesh union of marriage, and the children born of that union, serves as the primary image of God in creation. It is not an exaggeration to say that, from a biblical perspective, creation rises or falls on humanity's fidelity to its irreplaceable foundation in marriage.

My grandfather wrote my wife and me a letter just before we were married. What a gift of wisdom it was! In that letter he said that our marriage—in order to last—should be a "marriage made in heaven." I'd heard the expression before and always thought of it as a poetic conceit. But as I have read and reread his letter over the years, I believe he was reminding me that enduring marital love has to be seen as a calling originating in the heart of God. Marriage made in heaven gives heaven a place on earth, as it bears traces of the character of the heavenly God. God, who is faithful, just, loving, merciful, forgiving, kind, and life-creating, calls the married couple to reflect him. And in Jesus, who is the human face of God, we see in perfection just how extreme the divine character really is! From his self-emptying on the cross to the outpouring of the Holy Spirit on Pentecost, God's love for humanity surpasses all we could have ever asked for or imagined. And, for those of us crazy enough to entangle our faith in Jesus into our marital relationship, we allow something of God's self-wasting love to come and inhabit us.

MARRIAGE AS COVENANT

"Made in heaven" also means that marriage, created by a covenant-making God, is itself a covenant. The family that arises from the marital covenant is also, by extension, a covenant-bearing community. A covenant refers to a permanently binding and mutually beneficial relationship, sealed by an exchange of promises sworn under oath. These promises are guaranteed by a pledge of steadfast love, justice, and fidelity between the covenant partners. It's not just an exchange of gifts and services but an exchange of persons. I don't just give my wife "stuff" like money or emotional support, but I give her all of myself— heart, mind, body, soul—when I marry her.

> "MARRIAGE ISN'T JUST AN EXCHANGE OF 'STUFF.' IT'S AN EXCHANGE OF PERSONS."

The marital covenant, which reflects the covenant of God with humanity, pledges an exclusive, total, unbreakable, lifelong, faithful, and life-giving bond of mutual love between one man and one woman. Its binding obligations can only be dissolved by death and are witnessed and confirmed by God, who receives and seals our marital promises (see Matthew 19:6). This is radical monogamy born of an equally radical monotheistic faith: one God, one Lord, one baptism, one spouse. Monogamous marriage, and the family built on it, has been established by God as the privileged bearer of the divine–human covenant to the world. That said, those who break marital faith and divorce, or against whom marital faith is broken and are abandoned, can both—for different reasons—become powerful signs to the world of God's lavish mercy.

For Catholics, the most radical covenant-bearing "signs" are called "sacraments," those visible means of grace established by Jesus to open us to the infinite treasures that flow from his saving death and resurrection. We affirm in faith that Jesus has elevated natural marriage to the dignity of a sacrament. The sacrament of matrimony joins a baptized couple to Christ in his Church that they might participate together in the fullness of God's life and love poured into our hearts by the Holy Spirit. In both the Old and New Testaments, God's faithful and merciful covenant, love for humanity, is described as a nuptial love. Jesus, who came as the Bridegroom of Israel, perfects this covenant and invites men and women to unite their covenantal love to his. Paul, the author of Ephesians, makes this link dramatically explicit in 5:21–30, where the mutual submission (5:21) of husband and wife is stunningly redefined as mutual self-sacrificial love, patterned on Christ's sacrificial death, and ordered toward the holiness of the spouses. Sacraments are given to sanctify humanity, and sanctity means the perfection of Christlike love.

The disciples of Jesus, shaken by Jesus' shocking rejection of Moses' "hardhearted" rationale for divorce and his call for a return to the beginning (see Matthew 19:8), protested with a similar fear: "If that is the case of a man with his wife, it is better not to marry" (Matthew 19:10). I can't help but chuckle at their raw honesty! Jesus' response to their fearful objection is striking: "For human beings this is impossible, but for God all things are possible" (Matthew 19:26). In the Bible it's always God who makes and keeps covenants, while fallen human beings, from the very beginning of human history, can only seem to accept and then break those covenants. That's the premise of all salvation history, that humanity is destined to failure if God does not step in and intervene to save us from our powerlessness over sin and death. In the beginning, covenanted marriage was a pure gift of God to man and woman. It is no less the case that, in the new creation, covenanted marriage in Christ is a pure gift that must be received. Ask, seek, knock (see Matthew 7:7)!

MARRIAGE AS REAL LIFE

Christian marriage and family life is no abstract calling to an unreal ideal. Rather, it's an obedient response by people of faith to a divine vocation offered to real people by God, who became flesh and dwelt among us. That said, I would argue that Christian marriage is in some sense a genuinely "mystical" calling, meaning it opens to us privileged access to the experience of intimacy with the Holy Trinity. But I'd call this a "mysticism in the mud,"

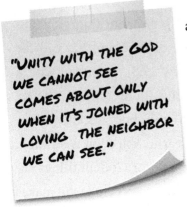

"UNITY WITH THE GOD WE CANNOT SEE COMES ABOUT ONLY WHEN IT'S JOINED WITH LOVING THE NEIGHBOR WE CAN SEE."

a down-to-earth spirituality that vividly reveals to us that unity with the Creator we cannot see comes about only when it's joined with loving the neighbor we can see (see 1 John 4:20)—in this case, loving our spouse and our children in the not-so-ideal conditions of real life.

Sacramental marriage involves us in gritty, daily, and real-life commitments carried out by real people who are struggling sinners. The vocation of marriage is very personal and particular. Marriage always has a face and a name, the face and name of your beloved. And you marry your beloved's past, present, and future; the good and the bad; the beautiful and the ugly: *everything*. Marital love is redemptive love. And, if God so wills, your marriage will give birth to a family composed of tiny new faces, with new names, each with a unique collection of strengths and weaknesses. Each of these new creations God entrusts to your marriage will be a new vocation spoken straight from the heart of God.

A seasoned and faith-filled father named Tim once shared with me this wisdom: "Tom, the keys to raising good children ares good friends, good books, good music, and your good marriage. A loving marriage is the hearth of the family, and a strong marriage is like an impenetrable wall that encircles children's tender souls. Put your marriage first. Protect it. Nurture it. You'll love your children best by loving Patti first. If they ask you, 'Do you love

Mom more than us?' you can answer, 'No, not more; just first.'
Saying marriage is a sacrament means your children get their first
experience of God in your marital love. When they're really little,
you are God. As they grow older, you get to lead them to know
and love God, and teach them to pray and hear his voice. And
then when they become adults, you get to walk with them to God.
They'll also learn from you both what it means to 'fail' in love. If
you keep it real and live it right, they'll learn that God's mercy
turns our failures into a deeper, sweeter, more mature capacity to
love. You both have to be rocks in the family, but to do that you
need to cling to Christ. And you need to be united—one mind,
one heart, a united front. But unity's the job of the Holy Spirit, so
turn to him often."

These words capture for me the heartbeat of the Church's
teaching on marriage-centered family life lived in Christ. For
Tim, who was theologically astute, getting the identity, vocation,
and mission of the family "right" was the most important task of
the Church.

The Christian family, built on the unshakable Christ-blessed
covenant love of husband and wife, is the first and most basic
communion of love in which an authentic community of persons,
marked by all the virtues that express a Christian character, can
develop. The family is defined above all by what St. Augustine called
the *ordo caritatis*, an ordering of relationships that is structured
by God's way of loving shown to us in Jesus. This "orderly love"
includes such things as honoring parents; welcoming, nurturing,
and educating children; revering and caring for the elderly;

forgiving and exercising patience with family members' sins and faults; exercising hospitality; and giving alms to the poor. It is only in a home adorned with "rightly ordered" love that every person welcomed into the family can be rightly recognized, accepted, and respected with dignity. The family is a school of Christian life whose doors open out into a sacred space where all can freely experience and practice genuine dialogue, selfless availability to others' needs, generous service, and the profound sense that we are our brother and sister's keeper.

THE MESS OF FAMILY LIFE

In many ways, one could say the whole Bible is the sacred history of God's dealing with families, and what a mess those families are! Ever since the sin of our first parents, family life has been disordered and dysfunctional, and God's relationship with human families has been as Savior and Redeemer who comes to reconcile an estranged spouse (see Ezekiel 16) and regather the scattered children of God (see John 11:52). Differences of dysfunction among families are only a matter of degree, as no family—save the Holy Family!—is an exception to the universal and home-wrecking dominion of sin.

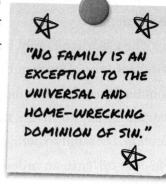

"NO FAMILY IS AN EXCEPTION TO THE UNIVERSAL AND HOME-WRECKING DOMINION OF SIN."

If you wonder if you're the only one from a messy family, just think about the stories of messed-up families that are woven through the biblical narrative! The story of the creation of Adam and Eve makes it clear that humanity is a single family, founded on a marriage, bound to God by a covenant imprinted by the fact that humanity is made in God's image and likeness. The story of the first humans' primordial sin—and the promise of salvation made by God—also makes clear that sin, and sin's remedy, is always a marital and family affair. The story of Cain and Abel further establishes a clear ethical standard that defines every deadly act of violence against another human being as fratricide, literally, the killing of a brother. But just noting the history of salvation is a very messy history of families called by God to receive his saving grace in a binding covenant, but again and again they break faith and fall into disaster, division, and death.

Think of the families stemming from Noah and his unnamed wife, Abram and Sarai/Hagar, Isaac and Rebecca, Jacob and Leah/Rachel, Joseph and Aseneth, David and his seven wives, Solomon and his 700 wives, and the majority of messed-up royal descendants

> "JESUS HAS COME TO SAVE HUMANITY BY RESTORING THE HUMAN FAMILY TO ITS ORIGINAL UNITY."

of the "house of David." These stories blend heroic examples of faith and obedience with scandalous, adulterous, murderous, polygamous, idolatrous marriages and families, torn by intrigue, strife, betrayal, lust, pride, envy, and revenge, breaking covenants with both God and neighbor. Saint Paul cried out, "Miserable one that I am! Who will deliver me from this mortal body?" (Romans

7:24). His answer is the hope of fallen humanity: "Thanks be to God through Jesus Christ our Lord!" (Romans 7:25). Jesus, the Bridegroom of Israel, has come to save humanity by restoring the human family to its original unity (Ephesians 3:14–15).

The New Testament presents a radical, divine response to the depth of damage that sin has inflicted on marriage and the family. But the greater destiny God has in store for humanity in Christ, adoption into the life of the Trinity, is equally radical. In redeeming us, Jesus dismantles the old defining structures of marriage and family life. He deconstructs the categories of birth, ethnicity, culture, race, or nationality and restructures them around himself. Faith in Jesus, and fidelity to his teaching, become the new unifying center of human identity, the new structuring principle of marriage and family life (see Mark 3:32–35; Luke 14:26; John 1:12–14; Galatians 3:28). Jesus' commandment of love, interpreted through the lens of his passion, becomes the new animating principle for marriage and family life (see Ephesians 5:21—6:9), even redefining the role of the slave in the household (see Philemon 15—16) and elevating the dignity of children from parental property to privileged icons of the kingdom (see Mark 10:13–16).

The New Testament also gives witness to the emergence of the "house church," which seems to refer to the homes of prominent Christians where the faithful would gather for celebrations of the Eucharist, fellowship, and instruction in the faith. In the age of the Fathers of the Church, this "house church" image was developed into a fuller theology of what St. Augustine called the "domestic church." This theology, more recently developed by St. John Paul

II in *Familiaris Consortio* (On the Role of the Christian Family in the Modern World), argues that marriage and family life include essential elements of the identity, vocation, and mission of the universal Church. The family is understood to be "the Church in miniature."

The family, like the Church as a whole, is a community of persons united in Christ through baptism, in service to life, sharing in the universal Church's mission to consecrate the world to God. In the family, vocations of service to the Church and the world are cultivated and discerned. In the family, the Gospel is proclaimed, taught, and enacted. In the family, divine mercy is sought in the form of repentance and dispensed in the form of forgiveness. In the family, God-given authority is exercised by virtuous self-mastery, in service to the right ordering of the household economy that extends out as leaven into the secular world.

FAMILY, BECOME WHAT YOU ARE

The sacramentally married couple will be tasked by God every day with "becoming what you are" (*FC* 17) and helping children to do the same. What are we? We know that we are created in God's image and likeness. We know that we are sinful and weak, powerless on our own to "be what we are." But we also know, by faith, that in Jesus our tarnished image has been polished. We have been recreated, forgiven, adopted as sons and daughters of God; reconciled to one another; and filled with the power of the Holy Spirit. But practically speaking, what does this mean for us?

We must strive daily to live this calling out as individuals, and then as a married couple, as parents, as members of an extended family, and as members of society. We strive to carry out God's will wherever we are, with the people we have been yoked to by obligation, in whatever are our circumstances. God, who is our merciful Redeemer, meets us in the mess and leads us along the way, helping us take the next best step toward his kingdom. Achieving holiness takes loads of prayer, trust, humility, patience, and an unrelenting commitment to love God and others with all we have to offer. The Church holds up for us the high and binding norms of marriage and family life—how God intends it to be—and asks that we strive to walk the way of perfection (see Matthew 5:48) even as we humbly accept our limitations and repent daily for our willful failures. The beauty of this vision is that it gives hope to sinful spouses and parents like me! Our sins, if given to God, can become opportunities for the superabundance of mercy to show its power (see Romans 5:20).

We are also called to cultivate a home for our children that is conducive to the formation of future saints. The Christian family educates children in a community of love and solidarity that hands on cultural, ethical, social, and religious values crucial for their personal development and for society as a whole. The family is the first school of social virtue and service to the common good, where children are empowered to grow in freedom and responsibility grounded in the full truth of the human person, so they might be equipped to carry out their personal vocations in the Church and society. A parent's love vivifies and guides all educational activities, "enriching it with the values of kindness, constancy, goodness, service, disinterestedness, and self-sacrifice that are the most precious fruit of love" (*Compendium of the Catechism of the Catholic Church*, 239). As parents, the contributions of both spouses will be equally necessary even if those roles are different. You have to work together, in harmony, and exercise your joint authority with respect and gentleness, as well as with firmness, consistency, wisdom, fairness, and with the total good of your child in mind.

Educating children is a tall order! But the beauty is that we never have to do it alone. We are part of a Church that is a family of families, a living "body" of Christ in which all are concerned for the well-being of all. At least that's our mission. Rely on the support of others, and pass on to those less fortunate than you the good things you have received. We are made in weakness that we might supply for one another.

THOMAS J. NEAL, PHD, is the academic dean and professor of spiritual theology at Notre Dame Seminary in New Orleans. He also leads retreats, workshops, and other catechetical events throughout the country. You can read more on his blog, nealobstat. wordpress.com.

CHURCH, FAMILY, AND WORKING TOGETHER:

OUR FAMILY'S RELATIONSHIP AND RESPONSIBILITY TO THE CHURCH

SEAN P. REYNOLDS, D.MIN

"WE'RE ON A MISSION FOR GOD."

So says the character Elwood Blues of the Blues Brothers in the cult classic movie of the same name. Mayhem ensues until Elwood and his brother Jake come up with the cash to save the orphanage where they grew up: mission accomplished!

"We're on a mission for God!" (absent the mayhem) could well be the words proclaimed by a newly married Catholic couple as they leave their wedding reception and head off into married life. That's what being married Catholic means—to be on a mission for God, and to lead your family in that mission.

PARENTS AND FAMILIES ARE MISSIONARY DISCIPLES

Pope Francis recently wrote, "Every Christian is a missionary to the extent that he or she has encountered the love

"WE'RE TRULY ON A MISSION FROM GOD AND THAT'S NO EXAGGERATION."

of God in Christ Jesus: we no longer say that we are 'disciples' and 'missionaries,' but rather that we are always 'missionary disciples'" (The Joy of the Gospel [*Evangelii Gaudium*], 120).

Catholic families are no exception. We're truly on a mission from God, and that's no exaggeration. Picture a rocket lifting a payload into orbit. Maybe that's not how you think about marriage and family, but it's a solid metaphor for the sacrament of matrimony. The payload is a fresh outpouring of love, and life, and good news into a world very much in need of them.

The wedding industry would have us think that all the fuss is about two people "in love." That's pretty shallow stuff compared to Catholic teaching on marriage and family, in which it's all about two becoming one in Christ, for the life of the world:

> Have among yourselves the same attitude that is also yours in Christ Jesus, who, though he was in the form of God, did not regard equality with God something to be grasped. Rather, he emptied himself, taking the form of a slave, coming in human likeness; and found human in appearance, he humbled himself, becoming obedient to death, even death on a cross (Philippians 2:5–8).

The Church teaches that the sacrament of matrimony is literally an opening of divine grace, the living power of God's Holy Spirit, made manifest in a lifetime of great and small acts of loving kindness. The grace of the sacrament is the rocket fuel that propels the couple in leading their family into their faith communities, neighborhoods, civic communities, and society as God-bearing emissaries of Christian love and joy.

St. John Paul II famously said, "As the family goes, so goes the nation and so goes the whole world in which we live." The day-to-day dedication of parents in shaping their homes and their children is, in fact, the foundational missionary work of peacemaking and justice seeking, with world-changing implications.

This perspective requires stepping back and getting the view from the balcony because so much of family life is daily, with far more baby steps than great strides. Perhaps grandparents have the best view when they witness their children and grandchildren extending the good news of their families outward into the world and forward in time. For young parents dealing with dirty diapers and runny noses, food allergies and sleep deprivation, it's far more an act of faith.

> "FAMILY LIFE IS DAILY, FILLED WITH MORE BABY STEPS THAN GREAT STRIDES."

FAMILIES ARE DOMESTIC CHURCHES OF THE HOME

The Church is ever ancient and ever new in its vision of the domestic churches of the home. Saint Paul, St. John Chrysostom, and St. Augustine set the standard in the first five centuries of the Church, saying that small home churches mirror the broader church, and vice versa. As the Church grew we began to lose the sense of that tradition and habitually began to think of the Church as a physical building, bishops and priests, or Mass on Sunday. However, that ancient tradition of "house churches" reemerged in the deliberations and documents of the Second Vatican Council (see Pastoral Constitution on the Church in the Modern World [*Gaudium et Spes*], 48), was further developed in Pope Paul VI's (What Is the New Evangelization, 1975), and then was firmly reestablished in St. John Paul II's *Familiaris Consortio* (1981).

Pope Francis now echoes Pope Paul VI, who broke new ground saying the Christian family should be "…an evangelizer of other families and of the neighborhood of which it forms a part…(in which) all members evangelize and are evangelized…" Paul VI in turn echoed Sts. Chrysostom and Augustine in saying that "there should be found in every Christian family the various aspects of the entire Church." In other words, as the institutional Catholic Church has ordained leaders of the faithful, so does the domestic church have leaders who are one in Christ: parents. Paul VI even went on to say those parents needn't both be Catholic: if they're united in a common baptism, they share the common mission of a family rooted in Christ.

ON THE ROLE OF THE FAMILY IN THE MODERN WORLD

After the 1980–81 global Synod of Bishops on the Family, Pope John Paul II wrote his apostolic exhortation *Familiaris Consortio*, which has constituted the basis of virtually every Catholic teaching on marriage and family thereafter. Following are the core tasks he deemed essential elements of the Catholic family's mission and an explanation for how to live these tasks in your own family.

Saint John Paul II was clear that there's plenty of hope and light in our families but that we're facing powerful challenges today that are profoundly different from those we've faced before. Whether through an insidious twisting of human freedom to selfish ends or through the objectification and depersonalization of human beings in a mass-market consumer economy, the result is the same: dehumanization. These core tasks set the bar high for Catholic families, but they are our best defense against these threats.

**TASK #1
FORMING A
COMMUNITY
OF PERSONS**

Because love is both the grounding and the calling of Christian families, we are to become communities of love in which the dignity of all is honored and respected. Women and men have equal dignity, with differing gifts. The dignity of children and the elderly is a precious gift. Anything that denies or rejects this dignity, such as pornography, breaks the sacred communion of family.

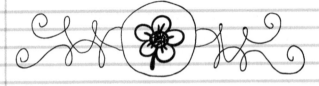

Continue to affirm the need for Christian marriages to be in harmony with God's plan for married life, the sanctity of life, the complementarity and necessity of both the unitive and procreative aspects of married sexuality, the immorality of contraception and sterilization as forms of birth control, and the dignity of life wherever that defense is needed.

**TASK #2
SERVING LIFE**

Because the family is the "first and vital cell of society," it plays an extraordinarily vital role in humanizing and personalizing broader society. As families, we are called to offer hospitality and care, especially to the poor and children in need of foster care or adoption. When necessary, we must band together into political associations in order to effect change or in defense of faith or family. (For a comprehensive list, see "The Charter of Family Rights," *Familiaris Consortio*, 46.)

TASK #3
PARTICIPATING IN THE DEVELOPMENT OF SOCIETY

Christian families are the Church "in miniature," so we also share in the three offices of Christ that form the substance of the broader Church: priest, prophet, and king. Prayer and worship are the centerpieces of the family role as "priest," and parents especially are called upon to ground their families in regular, deep, and meaningful prayer. As "king," families play a vital part in the structure of the Church as cells of the larger body of Christ and active participants in its ongoing life. The "prophetic" role of families lies in their mission to both the broader Church and the world, to be heralds of the Good News by being and living what they are: domestic churches of the home.

TASK #4
SHARING IN THE LIFE AND MISSION OF THE CHURCH

FAMILIES ARE SANCTIFIED AND SANCTIFIERS

The bishops of the United States brought home this vision of family in their pastoral message to families in 1991, *Follow the Way of Love*. It stands as a wonderful statement of our own bishops' care for families and their vision of what makes a domestic church. Some years earlier, they had published *A Family Perspective in Church and Society* with its companion piece *Families at the Center* as a framework for the U.S. Catholic Church's pastoral ministry with families. Both documents stand as testaments of the care, concern, and affection for Catholic families:

> We write to you as pastors and teachers in the Church, but we come to you as family members also. We are sons and brothers and uncles. We have known the commitment and sacrifices of a mother and father, the warmth of a family's care, the happiness and pain that are part of loving.... What you do in your family to create a community of love, to help each other to grow, and to serve those in need is critical, not only for your own sanctification but for the strength of society and our Church. It is a participation in the work of the Lord, a sharing in the mission of the Church. It is holy.
>
> *Follow the Way of Love*, 1991

We Catholics sometimes recoil from the notion that family life is holy because so often it seems anything but that. Family life is so hands on, so mundane, so very daily, how could it be holy? We're used to thinking of holiness in terms of priests and religious, or Mass, or what happens in a church building—not in our kitchens, basements, and bedrooms.

"FAMILY LIFE IS SO HANDS ON, SO MUNDANE, SO VERY DAILY, HOW COULD IT BE HOLY?"

Yet the bishops affirm over and over that God is love, and families that live in love, live in God, and God lives in them (see 1 John 4:9–11). This is the mission of Catholic families, and in many ways it's ground zero of the mission of Christ and the Church: to be, live, nurture, engender, multiply, develop, grow, and support love, because God is love.

That mission flows out of our baptism; is nourished at the eucharistic table; is realigned in the sacrament of reconciliation; is fortified with the power of the holy spirit in confirmation; and is commissioned for life in the sacrament of matrimony. That "way of love" leads us deeply into love within our families, and its reach goes far beyond our families as the Good News that we bear and simply have to share. The bishops say it clearly, and without qualification: "As Christian families, you not only belong to the Church, but your daily life is a true expression of the Church."

This pathway to holiness, this family journey with Christ, happens in countless ways, day to day. Here's a list adapted from *Follow the Way of Love* to get you thinking about what that holiness might look like in your family:

BELIEVE IN GOD.
In good times and bad,
in sickness and
in health.

LOVE.
Never giving up on love,
and help your children, and
everyone else, understand
that God is love.

FOSTER AUTHENTIC INTIMACY.
Take the intimacy you share
with your spouse and extend
it in appropriate ways to the
rest of the family and beyond.

EVANGELIZE.
Live the Gospel out loud and
with integrity so that people—
including your children—
understand where love, truth,
beauty, and goodness originate,
and how to access that source.

EDUCATE.
Continue growing and learning
about your faith, encourage
your family to develop habits
of lifelong learning and
spiritual growth.

PRAY.
Develop the habits and
disciplines of a deep and
regular life of prayer, both
individually and as a family.

SERVE.
Become a servant both within your family and to the community, especially to those who are hungry, poor, lonely, ill, or imprisoned.

FORGIVE.
Forgive as often as necessary to become blessed as peacemakers. Let the members of your family hear you say "I'm sorry" and "I forgive you" often.

 ## CELEBRATE.
Whenever the opportunity arises, show your joy in the wonders, gifts, and challenges of life God has given you.

WELCOME STRANGERS.
Open your home, especially to those without homes, such as immigrants, refugees, or the poor.

ACT JUSTLY.
Stand against racism, prejudice, and discrimination. Work to undo systemic injustices and social ills.

AFFIRM LIFE.
Respect human dignity, exercise nonviolence, and practice peacemaking.

NURTURE VOCATIONS.
Honor the extraordinary service of priests, religious, and deacons. Model the "sanctified" married life for your children.

Oppose that which destroys life such as abortion, euthanasia, unjust war, capital punishment, neighborhood and domestic violence, poverty and racism.

Trying to live this kind of family life might seem way out of reach, and no family is perfect. Most parents feel like they're doing all they can to just be somewhere in the neighborhood of adequate—and that's on a good day! So this list isn't provided as some kind of assessment, but to offer some specifics on what a family might strive for in following the way of love.

STAYING FOCUSED ON THE MISSION

"We're on a mission from God." That's how we began this chapter, and it's time to circle back to it. If you've seen *The Blues Brothers*, you know that Elwood and Jake Blues are flawed with good hearts. Aren't we all? Let's take some consolation from their story, that being on a mission from God doesn't require perfection, only faith and resolve.

We know that our families are called to an extraordinary evangelizing mission, to be what they are: authentic Catholic home churches. We also have a compelling and specific set of markers detailing what this unique form of the Church can look like, markers that are grounded in rock-solid Catholic teaching. So what will it take to make domestic churches of the home a reality in our parishes, neighborhoods, and communities?

There are two powerful impediments we'll need to reckon with. The first—which presents a grand opportunity—is that we're still uncovering the rich treasure of the domestic church. We're still learning how to do it. It also means that many, or perhaps most, of our people are either unaware of it, or pay lip service to it and then get on with business as usual. No shame, no blame.

That's where our history has brought us and the opportunity it extends to us.

This impediment is compounded by the ubiquitous consumer culture that has also shaped us and that in large part has shaped how we do church. So we're facing two big, interconnected realities: not only do we lack any robust recent history of Catholic house churches, but we also have a long-standing habit of relying on Catholic institutions, priests, and religious to "be holy" for us–and those institutions, priests, and religious in turn have a long-standing history of being so relied upon.

The result is that our default instincts are to defer to the pastor, the school, the religion teacher, the DRE, or the youth minister, because when we think of "Church" that's what we picture: "…the Church is their job, so leave it to the professionals!" Conversely, our Church leaders and institutions have equally been shaped so as to expect to be deferred to and delegated to: "…The Church is our job, so leave it to us!"

We call plumbers, see doctors, trust teachers and schools, demand reliable and courteous service, and expect to get what we pay for. Trouble is, faith, church, love, God, and spirit all operate out of a very different economy. In the faith economy, our only reasonable expectations are that God will be faithful as we follow Jesus to the cross, into the tomb, and miraculously out again! What's been termed the "consumer-provider" model of church can only fail, because it's church only in name.

All those centuries that Catholic teaching on the domestic church was underemphasized have shaped us into pastors, parishes, and schools—and parents, grandparents, and children—with a lopsided set of expectations about where "the Church" is and who is responsible for it. In short, "missionary discipleship" runs counter to some of our deepest instincts as U.S. consumers. As a result we have quite a bit of unlearning to do before we'll be able to get much traction at all on our vision of the domestic church of the home.

Nurturing the vision of the domestic church is a centerpiece of the national Strong Catholic Families movement, and leaders of that movement are guided by what's called the **E5 Change Model.** It was developed as a strategic response to these two intersecting impediments/opportunities and can help guide you as you work with your parish and in your home to strengthen the ties between faith and family.

EVOKE: In order for any change to happen, people need to be convinced that the status quo is unacceptable and that change absolutely has to happen. In other words, we need compelling evidence that the current consumer-provider model of church isn't working.

Recent and ongoing research into the faith of Catholic children, youth, and young adults sadly provides us with far more compelling evidence than we need. The best research we have from Pew, Gallup, CARA, the National Study of Youth & Religion, and so forth, add up to one over-arching conclusion: the status quo isn't working well at all for us Catholics, and we need to become a Church in which parents and families are primary. We need to put the development of the domestic church on the fast track.

ENVISION: Church leaders and parents need a clear and compelling vision of a viable, rich, and wonderful alternative to the consumer-provider model. In other words, we need precisely what the Second Vatican Council, our recent popes, and our magisterial Church teaching all have called for: the domestic church!

EQUIP: If church leaders are going to be useful to our domestic churches, they will need to get equipped with a very different set of resources, programs, homilies, and priorities than they're used to. Why? Because most of our church leaders are just as used to the consumer-provider model of church as are parents and families, or maybe more.

Most of our parishes provide preparation for the sacrament of baptism, including one or two fairly brief meetings with a deacon or priest prior to the sacrament. Then nothing. If we're serious about equipping the domestic church, most of our pastoral planning and attention needs to focus on what happens after the sacrament. We'll be partnering with young parents and families, building loving and trusting relationships with them, and providing them lots of support, prayer, encouragement, and resources.

EVOLVE: Both church leadership and parents/families will evolve into Catholic communities where the domestic church becomes the norm instead of the exception. In such places, both the domestic churches and the mother Church will more fruitfully pursue their common mission of evangelization.

EVANGELIZE: Even though it's the fifth and final step, evangelization is infused in all five steps. Every effort to evoke a sense of urgency for the domestic church must be accompanied by an invitation to more deeply encounter the living Christ.

At this point you might ask: Isn't there an easier way? Can't I just buy a book, take a course, or do an online program?

Very few of us were raised in domestic churches. Most of us grew up in homes with the assumption that "the Church" is "at church." So we learned that to "be holy" is to be at church. We learned to expect our clergy and religious, our institutions, schools, parishes, and church agencies to be the Church.

Spouses, consider this: Did you think as you awoke this morning in bed next to your beloved, "How great it is to go to bed and get up in church?"

Children, consider this: When you were complaining about "going to church," were you complaining about being at home with your parents and families? Did it ever occur to you that you *are* the Church, and your parents are its leaders and pastors?

Catholic parents, consider this: That "going to church" on most days means coming home. If you're sold on that idea, consider this: are you praying, preparing, and planning for your church of the home, as you would expect your pastor and the staff to do at the parish? Are you the primary influence on the faith of your children, or have you delegated that to others?

We've got work to do. Let's get to it.
We're on a mission from God.

SEAN P. REYNOLDS, D. MIN, is director of the office of youth ministry of the Archdiocese of Cincinnati. He holds degrees in theology and in community organization and development. He also is a sought-after speaker and workshop presenter.

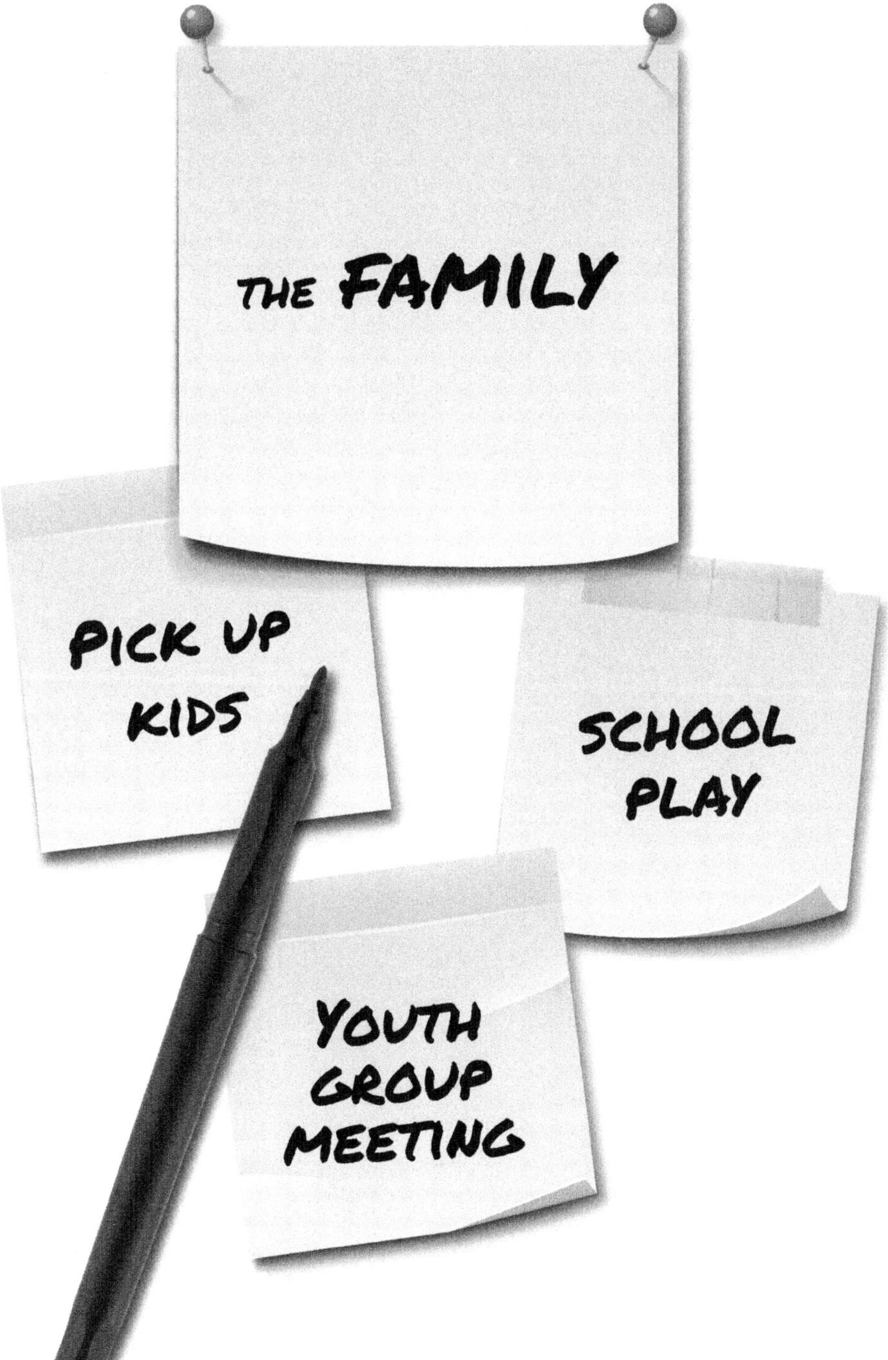
THE FAMILY
PICK UP KIDS
SCHOOL PLAY
YOUTH GROUP MEETING

Changing Times, Changing Roles, Same Family:

●● ● ● ● ● ● ● ●

The Catholic Vision of Family Life in the 21st Century

Dr. Gregory Popcak

Family life has changed radically over the past few decades,

and there is no denying that Catholics have been caught up in the cultural whirlwind. By and large, our current culture is not only unreceptive to the Church's views on marriage and family life but it is often also intent on condemning it as oppressive, discriminatory, outdated, undesirable, and—at any rate—impossible to live up to. Can the Catholic vision of family life remain relevant in this brave new world? Is there a place for Catholic families in the modern world? If so, what does that place look like? Is it even possible to hold on to a Catholic vision of family life in the midst of the cultural storm that is raging against family life as a whole?

"CAN THE CATHOLIC VISION OF FAMILY LIFE REMAIN RELEVANT IN THIS BRAVE NEW WORLD?"

CATHOLIC FAMILIES: ACCEPTING OUR PROPHETIC MISSION

I believe the answer to these questions is a resounding "yes." Now, more than ever, Catholic families must learn to assert their unique identity as prophetic witness and live that identity more boldly, courageously, and grace-fully than ever! Yes, our social context has changed, but our mission has not. God still longs to call all people to himself (John 12:32) and, if we let him, he intends to use the radical witness of the Catholic family to do it.

These are brave words, especially when it seems like so many Catholics are unaware that the Church even proposes a unique vision of family life. Add to this the fact that so few people have any personal experience of a stable family life and it is little wonder that many Catholics feel more than a little shell-shocked. Pope Francis' call for an Extraordinary Synod to address the challenges of evangelizing the family sheds light on the seriousness of the challenge before us. To get a sense of the magnitude of the shift we're contending with, let's take a brief look at family life then and now. The superscripts that follow refer to resources listed at the end of this book.

ONCE UPON A TIME...

Throughout the 1950s and 1960s, Catholic families, like nearly 80 percent of all American families, were predominantly traditional in structure. A father served as the primary breadwinner and the mother stayed at home.[1] Family life may not have been blissful all the time, but it was considerably more stable. Up through the early 1970s, the majority of married couples stayed together for life, and the divorce rate was lower than 25 percent. Cohabitation rates were as low as 1 percent[2]. On average, parents had about four children[3], and fewer than 5 percent of children were born out of wedlock[4]. Likewise, about 62 percent of Catholics attended Mass weekly through the late 1960s[5].

INTO THE BRAVE NEW WORLD

Today the picture is remarkably different. About 48 percent of women have cohabited with a boyfriend before marrying their current spouse[6]. Since the advent of no-fault divorce legislation in the 1970s, the divorce rate for Catholics as a whole is similar to the general population's, which hovers between 40 percent and 50 percent[7]. In this third generation of the culture of divorce, it is not unusual for a young adult to have both divorced parents and divorced grandparents with little to no personal experience of long-term, intact family life. If there is any good news, it is that Catholic couples who attend Mass exhibit much greater marital stability than the general population (the divorce rate for weekly Mass attendees is in the 5 percent to 15 percent range). Unfortunately, only 20 percent of Catholics go to Mass every week[8].

If the overall stability of the family has changed, so has its makeup. The size of today's average family has shrunk 50 percent to about two children. Roughly 41 percent of all children are now born to unmarried women and about half of children (44 percent) have a step-sibling[9]. In general, parents today are older, with women regularly delaying childbearing until their thirties. Additionally, because of both increased work opportunities for women and economic necessity, 70 percent mothers now work outside the home[10].

THE MODERN FAMILY: WORKING WITHOUT A NET

Although these statistics may not be surprising, the significance of these changes with regard to evangelizing the culture is lost on many. In light of this cultural milieu, even intact, faithful families are negatively impacted. For the most part, family life has been redefined as a collection of individuals living under the same roof and sharing a data plan. Even so-called "normal" families are struggling under the weight of the cultural expectation that extracurricular activities should now provide the socialization and sense of meaning that family life used to impart. Parents and children of even the healthiest families are constantly tempted to pursue activities like work, sports, and technology over emotional and spiritual intimacy through family dinners, family time, and family prayer and worship.

"FAMILY LIFE HAS BEEN REDEFINED AS A COLLECTION OF INDIVIDUALS LIVING UNDER THE SAME ROOF AND SHARING A DATA PLAN."

During the Extraordinary Synod on the Family held in 2014, there was much discussion about how the Church might respond to the needs of the "irregular family"; that is, families impacted by divorce, cohabitation, single-parent households, and so forth. As both necessary and well-intentioned as these conversations may be, this focus fails to grasp that in the modern world virtually every family is irregular. These changes necessitate that the Church find radical new ways to form and support families.

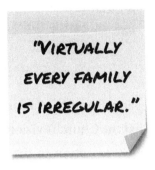

"VIRTUALLY EVERY FAMILY IS IRREGULAR."

In past generations, it was possible to adopt a more catechetical approach to marriage and family education in the Church. The prevailing family-friendly culture did the hard work of drawing the boundaries that defined the nature and the mores of family life. With some exceptions, the Church could simply inform and encourage families to become better at what they were already doing. Today's families, however, must function without either a clearly defined blueprint for what a strong family looks like or a cultural safety net to catch them if they fall. Without social support and reliable parental modeling, simple catechetical/informational approaches to family formation are doomed to fail. Information is not enough. Actual formation, mentoring, and discipleship is needed to teach people the basic steps of healthy family life. Moreover, the cultural landscape has changed to the degree that the majority of families living in the twenty-first century simply do not have sufficient grounding in what a basic,

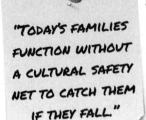

"TODAY'S FAMILIES FUNCTION WITHOUT A CULTURAL SAFETY NET TO CATCH THEM IF THEY FALL."

stable family life resembles to be able to make the leap to applying their faith to family life. Using a merely catechetical approach to convey the ins and outs of faithful family life is like asking people to learn juggling from a textbook.

These facts necessitate a new approach to evangelizing the family that shows, rather than tells, the world that the Church's vision of family life is a vital, workable, desirable, positive option to the world's alternative of personal fulfillment though radical cultural isolation.

SPIRITUAL AMBIVALENCE: WHY HEALTHY FAMILIES ARE THE ANSWER

Saint John Paul II observed this problem and he responded in two powerful ways by presenting his *Theology of the Body (TOB)* and by proclaiming the New Evangelization. Both of these concepts go hand in hand to the degree that discussing the New Evangelization without a thorough sense of the *TOB* is, in effect, attempting to put new wine into the same old wineskins (Mark 2:22). The *TOB* presents a phenomenological (experience-based) approach to understanding God's intention for human relationships. It proposes a means of communicating God's vision of love, marriage, and family life to the post-modern world using its own language; a language whose vocabulary is "experience" and whose syntax is "relationship."

Likewise, the New Evangelization is specifically concerned

with bringing the post-modern person to Christ. Because the post-modern world defines reality in terms of feelings and experience rather than objective truth, the post-modern person has little ability to understand traditional natural-law reasoning. Furthermore, the average person raised in the post-modern era has become radically disillusioned with both family life and other social institutions (for example, political and religious). Because of this, the contemporary individual's experience of faith—understood as the innate, human drive to seek meaning and spiritual significance[11]—has largely been displaced by irony, doubt, and ambivalence. Today's spiritual "seeker" is often not on a journey toward an ultimate spiritual home as much as he or she is trapped in a state of perpetual spiritual wandering[12]. Such a person often attends one church after another, sampling this, tasting that, but never really settling in or committing to a single, coherent, spiritual path. This ambivalence is the defining characteristic of the growing category of people who are "spiritual but not religious."

The preeminent psychologist of religion, Dr. Ken Pargament argues that the spiritual ambivalence I am describing here is rooted in the family[13], specifically, in the child's inability to idealize parents or other adults in authority in his or her life (such as teachers, pastors, coaches). Of course, all children come to realize that adults are fallible, and discovering this is necessary for a healthy transition to adulthood. But Pargament's research shows that if this realization comes too soon—because the adults in children's lives have been consistently unavailable, disconnected, distracted, selfish, out of touch, neglectful, or abusive—children never really learn who they can reliably follow or to whom they can consistently turn for guidance except themselves. Ultimately, this translates into an ambivalence toward all institutions traditionally charged with helping people find meaning and significance.

Elizabeth Marquardt observed a similar dynamic in her groundbreaking work on the spiritual lives of children of divorce[14]. Even in so-called "good divorces" (that is, low-conflict divorces when the children maintain a good relationship with both parents), the fact that children are constantly moving back and forth between two often very different worlds (the mother's and the father's) that never come together in any meaningful way except inside the children's own heads, results in their never learning to trust anyone but themselves to help make sense of life.

WORDS, WORDS, WORDS...

How do we evangelize such a person? Clearly, mere words won't work. Saint Paul said, "faith comes from what is heard" (Romans 10:17), but for the post-modern person, the more relevant Scripture is St. James' proclamation that "faith of itself, if it does not have works, is dead" (James

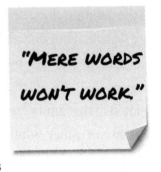

"MERE WORDS WON'T WORK."

2:17). The post-modern individual has heard too many words: "You can trust me"...."I will always be here for you"...."I will always love you"...."You can count on me." In most cases, for the individual coming up in the post-modern world of cohabitation, no-fault divorce, serial monogamy, fatherlessness, and serial hooking up, these words are just that, empty words.

As Pope Francis has observed, such a person needs an encounter with people for whom the Catholic vision of love, marriage, and family is making a tangible, positive difference[15]. This is where the Catholic vision of family life comes into play. The institutional Church must do everything possible to practically support the mission work that God has given Catholic families to do, that is, to be a tangible witness to the positive and permanent nature of God's love in the world. It is the family that is the school of love (see the *Catechism of the Catholic Church*, 1657). In the New Evangelization, the Church must empower Catholic families to take center stage in its efforts to bring the world to Christ, because it is primarily through the witness of the Catholic family that the average person will most likely have his or her first personal encounter with the kind of love God wants to share with each of us, a love that is free, total, faithful, and fruitful. Just as it is the role of the ministerial priesthood to consecrate the host so that it may become the precious Body of Christ, it is the role of the common priesthood of the family to consecrate the human person's experience of relationship so that each husband, wife, parent, and child may be prepared to become part of the loving reality that is the mystical body of Christ.

CLARIFYING THE VISION

So what is this unique, positive vision of family life the Church offers the world? The Gospel of Life (*Evangelium Vitae*) presents what I consider the mission statement for Catholic families. In it, families are called to ground their lives in the pursuit of "authentic freedom, actualized in the sincere gift of self" and to cultivate, in all their interactions, "respect for others, a sense of justice, cordial openness, dialogue, generous service, solidarity and all the other values which help people to live life as a gift" (*EV* 92*)*.

Imagine the powerful impact such a family could have on each other's hearts and the hearts of those who encountered them! It can be tempting to say that these ideals are too lofty, but that would be missing the point. True, only Christ can accomplish this vision in our lives, but even our mere pursuit of this vision is stunning enough for the world to take notice. To

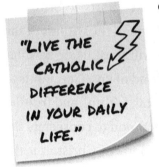

encounter Christians who believe in this vision of love enough to allow it to form the way they live their lives as husband, wife, parents, and children through good times and bad, sickness and health, wealth and poverty is a transformational experience.

THE FIVE "MARKS" OF THE CATHOLIC FAMILY

But how do Catholic families put this vision into practice? My wife and I discuss this question extensively in our various books on marriage and family life, particularly *Parenting With Grace,* but if we had to develop a simple list of foundational principles, we would suggest that the Catholic family must be known by following five "marks." Although the following list is not exhaustive, these five traits, drawn from our book *Discovering God Together,* serve as an excellent primer empowering families to live the Catholic difference in their daily lives.

CATHOLIC FAMILIES WORSHIP TOGETHER

The Eucharist is the source of our love and the sign of the intimacy to which we are called. Therefore, as a family, we attend Mass together on Sundays and holy days (and at other times as we are able) and actively participate in the sacramental life of the Church.

As part of this participation, we recognize that because we are fallen, we struggle to be the loving communities we are called to be. Therefore, as a family, we regularly go to confession (recommended monthly) to seek God's healing and grace so we might better live his vision of love in our lives and homes.

CATHOLIC FAMILIES PRAY TOGETHER

The Church refers to families as "the domestic church" because family life is where the faith is supposed to be lived out every day. Catholic families are called to love each other not only with their human love but also with the love that flows from God's own heart. As Catholic families, we recognize that we cannot love one another as God loves us unless we ask him—*together*—to teach us what this means. Therefore, in addition to both our individual prayer life and our worship with our parish communities, we gather together both as husband and wife and also as a family for prayer each day.

Use these opportunities to:

Don't pray in the manner of "checking off a box" but in an honest, heartfelt manner that leads to deeper intimacy with God and each other.

- **PRAISE AND THANK GOD FOR HIS BLESSINGS.**
- **ASK FORGIVENESS FOR THE TIMES YOU DID NOT LOVE GOD AND EACH OTHER AS YOU OUGHT.**
- **ASK GOD FOR THE GRACE TO LOVE EACH OTHER AND THE WORLD BETTER.**
- **SEEK GOD'S WILL FOR YOUR LIFE.**
- **PRAY FOR BOTH YOUR NEEDS AND THE NEEDS OF THE FAMILY OF GOD.**

3

CATHOLIC FAMILIES ARE CALLED TO INTIMACY

The Christian life is first and foremost a call to intimate communion. As St. Jean Vianney said, "Prayer is nothing less than union with God."

We recognize that families are schools of love (*Catechism of the Catholic Church*, 1657) where we learn how to love God and each other with our whole hearts, minds, souls, and strength (Luke 10:27). Therefore, as a family, we constantly challenge ourselves to discover new ways to be even more open with and loving to each other as husband and wife, parents and children.

We recognize that children are a visible sign of the loving union between husband and wife, and we work to make this a reality in our homes both in our openness to life and by working hard on the quality of our relationships with each other. Further, we cultivate marriage and parenting practices that make each member of the family willingly open up to one another and seek to freely give themselves to create a deeper "community of love" and practice all the virtues that help us live life as a gift. For instance, we choose loving guidance approaches to discipline that focus on teaching and rewarding good behavior and virtues as opposed to more negative and reactive approaches that simply punish bad behavior. We schedule regular one-on-one time with each family member so we can get to know each other's thoughts, feelings, and desires on the deepest level possible. And we take an active interest in all the things that each family member find true, good, and beautiful even when that interest doesn't come naturally to us.

CATHOLIC FAMILIES PUT FAMILY FIRST

We recognize that, because our family relationships are the primary vehicle God uses to perfect us and challenge us to become everything we were created to be, family life itself is the most important activity in our week. To protect the intimacy we are called to cultivate as the domestic church, we recognize the importance of regular family rituals that promote opportunities to work, play, talk, and pray together and we are intentional about creating and protecting those activities. We hold these activities as sacred rituals of the domestic church and value them over all other activities that would seek to compete with them.

If you're working to build more family time into your weekly schedule here are some things you can try:

- FAMILY DINNERS

- TIME FOR FAMILY PRAYER AND WORSHIP

- A GAME NIGHT OR FAMILY DAY

- SCHEDULE TIME FOR COMMUNICATION AND RELATIONSHIP BUILDING

THE CATHOLIC FAMILY IS A WITNESS AND SIGN

We recognize that God wants to change the world through our families. We allow ourselves to be part of his plan for changing the world in two ways. First, we do this by striving to exhibit the closeness, love, and intimacy that every human heart longs for. We must show the world that this love is a possibility worth striving for and should be shown in good times and bad, in sickness and in health, for richer or poorer.

Second, we will carry this love outside the home by serving the world-at-large in a manner that is responsible and respects the integrity of our family relationships. We do this by committing ourselves and our families to the intentional practice of all the corporal and spiritual works of mercy within the home and outside of it. To this end, the ways we, as a family, are trying to fulfill this responsibility will be a regular topic of conversation in our homes.

FAMILIES: GO OUT AND "MAKE A FUSS"

In his opening address at the 2013 World Youth Day, Pope Francis famously called the faithful to "make a fuss," that is, to challenge the established order in an active intentional effort to call the world to Christ. That is exactly what a family dedicated to living

> "YOUR FAMILY CAN BECOME A PROPHETIC WITNESS, CALLING THE WORLD TO CHRIST."

these proposed five marks of a Catholic family would do. Simply by inviting friends to your home for dinner or going out to shop for groceries or attending a school event, you are working diligently each day to live out these principles and challenge the world's impoverished assumptions about family life. Your family can become a prophetic witness, calling the world to Christ by virtue of the love that dwells in your heart and your home.

The Church needs such families. The world needs such families. With God's grace, yours can be the kind of family that draws others to Christ through your loving example, not because you have achieved perfection (or are good at pretending that you have), but because you are willing to sit at the feet of the Master and learn to care for each other with the love that comes from God's own heart. It is my prayer that as you practice the steps of God's love in your family, your witness would inspire all those you meet to discover your "secret," which is nothing less than Jesus Christ himself.

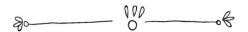

DR. GREGORY POPCAK, the founder of the Pastoral Solutions Institute, is the author of many books on marriage and family life, including *For Better...FOREVER!*, *Parenting With Grace,* and *Holy Sex!* A pastoral counselor and host of *More2Life Radio,* he also serves as an adjunct professor of psychology and graduate theology at Franciscan University of Steubenville (Ohio). Please visit him at CatholicCounselors.com.

FAITH, FAMILY, AND
FINDING THE TIME:

HOW TO GET EVERYONE
IN YOUR FAMILY
FOCUSED ON FAITH

LISA M. HENDEY

WHAT DOES A CATHOLIC MOM HAVE TO SAY?

I often wish I had the means to go back in time and visit with myself as a young mother. I would offer that young lady a bit of perspective on what her priorities should be. When I remember those days now, filled with toddlers and temper tantrums (thrown as often by me as by my two precious sons Eric and Adam), it's tempting to wish for a "do over." I'm equally as certain that I'll wish for that same type of wisdom years from now when I'm an aging grandmother looking back on these days of parenting young adults. Although embracing my vocation as a Catholic mom has never been simple, it has, without a doubt, been the greatest joy of my life.

I'd like to enter this conversation with you by offering a stern caveat that I do not consider myself by any means to be an expert on the topic of the domestic church. Even after almost thirty years, our family is still very much a work-in-progress. What I know of this amazing vocation has come to me by watching my own parents successfully raise five of us and our spouses in the faith, by interacting on a daily basis with parents around the world via my internet-based apostolate, and by studying the teachings of our Catholic Church on this most important of topics.

Even after nearly a quarter-century spent parenting, I am still a novice who loves to linger at the feet of the paramount mother, the Blessed Virgin Mary. Although that may seem to be a lofty benchmark, I turn to Jesus' mom for her example, as well as to her most chaste spouse, St. Joseph, because they also likely grappled with their own trials in understanding the role of faith in their family. In Catholic families, it's easy to fall prey to the temptation to look with envy or despair at other families and assume they never face the challenges we do in our own homes. The more I mature in my understanding of our faith, the more I recognize that all families deal with their own trials and tribulations. For us to find joy and peace in our own vocation as Catholic parents, we must stop our comparisons and begin to embrace our own unique gifts and circumstances.

"TURN TO MARY AND JOSEPH BECAUSE THEY TOO GRAPPLED WITH THEIR UNDERSTANDING OF FAITH IN THEIR FAMILY."

What connects most Catholic parents is our deeply held faith in the teachings of our Church, as well as our sincere desire to pass along this same gift to our children. When we bring our children forth for baptism, we vow solemnly to commit ourselves to the task of raising these young souls in the faith. This includes the promise to make family Mass attendance a weekly priority, to see to the religious education of our children, and to set an example of Christlike love and values for them by our own endeavors to live the faith. We promise verbally as we stand before the baptismal font to teach these young souls to keep God's commandments as Christ taught us, by loving God and our neighbor.

How simple that vow feels when we hold a precious white-garbed infant in our arms, supported by loving godparents and with the delicious aroma of the chrism oils still fresh in the air. And yet, how challenging that promise can feel when we attempt to quiet a petulant toddler in the midst of a consecration or coax a defiant teen to participate in the Mass when their peers have all walked away. Yet, as Catholic parents, we rest assured in the knowledge that we do not undergo the challenges of the domestic church alone.

> **As the *Catechism of the Catholic Church* teaches us:**
> In our own time, in a world often alien and even hostile to faith, believing families are of primary importance as centers of living, radiant faith. For this reason the Second Vatican Council, using an ancient expression, calls the family the *Ecclesia domestica.* [continued on next page]

It is in the bosom of the family that parents are "by word and example...the first heralds of the faith with regard to their children" (*CCC* 1656).

It is here that the father of the family, the mother, children, and all members of the family exercise the priesthood of the baptized in a privileged way "by the reception of the sacraments, prayer and thanksgiving, the witness of a holy life, and self-denial and active charity" (*CCC* 1656). Thus the home is the first school of Christian life and "a school for human enrichment" (*CCC* 1657). Here one learns endurance and the joy of work, fraternal love, generous—even repeated—forgiveness, and above all divine worship in prayer and the offering of one's life.

With both the Church as our guide and the examples of the communion of saints as our role models, prioritizing faith in our families can create a joy of living out the gospel in our homes that will enable us to weather even the greatest storms. Faith is not only a creed we profess from the depths of our heart but also a cement that bonds us to one another in a way that many families who lack it will never truly understand. Our unity of belief in the promises of Christ becomes our family's answer to the challenge issued in 1 Peter 3:15 to "always be ready to give an explanation to anyone who asks you for a reason" for the hope that sets us apart.

"FAITH IS NOT ONLY A CREED WE PROFESS, BUT A CEMENT THAT BONDS US TO ONE ANOTHER."

EUCHARIST AT THE CORE OF OUR FAMILIES

In today's world, it seems countercultural to live a family life centered on the Catholic faith and the Eucharist. While recent studies show one quarter of the adults in the United States identify themselves as Catholic, we also know that fewer than 25 percent of Catholics say they attend Mass weekly. Perhaps you've experienced the unusual situation of a parish nearly empty on a typical Sunday, but filled to the brim for back-to-back Ash Wednesday services. Even some parents who pay for a Catholic school education prioritize travel with sports teams over Mass attendance as a family. Without the Eucharist as the source and summit of our faith, families begin to lose the very core of what makes them truly Catholic.

When families come to me to discuss the challenges they are facing in their Catholic homes, one of the most frequent questions I ask is, "Do you make attendance at Mass as a family a priority in your life?" All too often, my question is met with a variety of excuses about busyness, children who refuse to attend, or work priorities that make Mass attendance "impossible." Believe me when I tell you that I can definitely relate to being the mother who finds herself alone in the pew with two rowdy toddlers on the receiving end of glares from elderly parishioners. (Perhaps that's why these days I go out of my way to try to offer a word of encouragement to any young family I meet at Mass.)

Without the centrality of the Eucharist as the core foundational value of our families, we are lost. Until we commit ourselves to not only attending Mass together as a family but also to finding a role of true service for ourselves and our children in our parishes, church will never feel like the second "home" it is intended to be.

MAKING THE CHANGE

When I was a young adult and new mother, I struggled with the sensation that I was not getting anything out of Sunday Mass. I came and went feeling unfulfilled and alone. In those days, before my husband, Greg, entered the Catholic Church through RCIA, I knew that Sunday Mass was the most critical component of helping our little domestic church to grow. But I hadn't yet learned that Mass was not a "consumer" experience. I complained far too often that the parishes we chose were "unwelcoming." It wasn't until I learned that I had a responsibility to my parish to be more than just someone who showed up on Sunday expecting to be served that things changed.

If family Mass attendance is to be the glue that truly binds our families together, then an unwavering belief in the Real Presence of Jesus Christ in the Eucharist absolutely must be what sets our homes apart. We Catholic families simply must believe that when we receive holy Communion together on Sundays (and hopefully on other days of the week as well) we are united even more perfectly not only with one another but also with our Creator.

Gifted homilists may come and go in our parishes. Liturgical music may be beautiful, or not. What will never waver in our parish homes is the Real Presence of Jesus Christ in the Eucharist. For this reason, we must consistently lead our children into an ever-deepening encounter with the Church by participating in

Mass. We must also model for our children our deep desire to encounter Jesus in the gift of holy Communion.

From an early age, our babies watch and learn from us. When we prepare our hearts for Mass by reading and pondering the Liturgy of the Word in advance, when we dress for Mass as the highlight of our week, when we arrive early and sit in the front of church to more fully encounter the liturgy, and when we reverently go forward to receive Christ in the Eucharist, our actions underscore the words we profess in the Creed.

Being a family of faith does not end when we leave the church parking lot. Our Catholic faith calls us to not only listen to the Gospel but also to live it. We must, at every juncture, be willing to see the face of Jesus Christ in those around us, within our own homes, in the needy of our community, and in a world where so many live without the most basic necessities.

"BEING A FAMILY OF FAITH DOES NOT END WHEN WE LEAVE THE CHURCH PARKING LOT."

EVERY FAMILY MEMBER MATTERS

Families come in all shapes and sizes. In today's world, we can no longer assume that a Catholic family fits the traditional mold of two parents and multiple children. Now more than ever, our churches contain families with single parents, families with many or no children, families where parents have divorced or separated, families with foster or adoptive children, and families of multiple generations living within the same home.

Regardless of how many members a family has, one thing

holds true: every family member matters. Especially within families of faith, it is clear that each person in a family unit plays a unique role in drawing his or her relatives into closer relationship with God.

A *NEWBORN INFANT* opens the hearts of her joy-filled parents to the blessing and miracle of new life.

A *RAMBUNCTIOUS TODDLER* teaches his siblings and parents about patience and perseverance.

A devout *ELEMENTARY SCHOOL CHILD* hungering for her sacraments offers a beautiful lesson for her parents about never taking for granted the gift of reconciliation or holy Communion.

A *PETULANT TEENAGER* can lead his parents to an ever-deepening understanding of the nature of unconditional love.

A *YOUNG ADULT CHILD* leads her parents to develop trust in God's divine will for each of us.

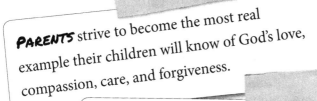

PARENTS strive to become the most real example their children will know of God's love, compassion, care, and forgiveness.

Even the experience of caring for and interacting with **CHILDREN WITH SPECIAL NEEDS**, for an **INFIRM RELATIVE**, or a **BELOVED GRANDPARENT** in the final stages of life can cultivate within us the ability to see the face of Jesus Christ in those most fragile of our loved ones.

In our homes, every family member takes a turn loving and being loved, forgiving, accepting forgiveness, serving and being served. Parents learn to rely not only upon one another for support and strength but also upon the often unwavering faith of their children to see the omnipresence of God with simple eyes and hearts unscarred by disappointment and loss. Just as we marvel at the fact that a young Christ Child could teach his parents about his heavenly Father, we must concede that our own children have the capacity to lead us into an ever deepening love for the one who fashioned us into being.

CULTIVATING FAITH IN YOUR DOMESTIC CHURCH

For some families, living out the faith at home comes easily. They may come from a long line of relatives whose faith has remained unwavering through the tests of time. But other families, for many different reasons, may find themselves struggling to cultivate a culture of faith or to build their own unique domestic church.

Such was certainly the case in our home. Although I was raised in an active Catholic family, my husband, Greg, was not brought up attending church on a regular basis. When we married, I vowed to raise our children in the Catholic Church. Greg consented to this agreement, but it was clear to me early on that if our sons were to know and love the Church, the responsibility would be mine. With Greg's full support, I began to commit myself fully to bringing my faith into our home. But those early years proved to be a struggle. I felt lonely, overwhelmed, and never "holy enough" for the task of being the primary faith formator of my children. These concerns led to an online search for resources that ultimately motivated me to begin my website, CatholicMom. com. I did not launch the site thinking I had all the answers. In fact, what I hoped to build—and am still working toward fifteen years later—is a community of mothers like myself who could focus together on how to cultivate, cherish, and treasure our Catholic faith in our homes. Even now, with my husband having come

> "I FELT LONELY, OVERWHELMED, AND NEVER 'HOLY ENOUGH' FOR THE TASK OF BEING THE PRIMARY FAITH FORMATOR OF MY CHILDREN."

into the Church seventeen years into our marriage, I continue to learn something new every day about what it means to live out the faith in our family.

LIVE BY EXAMPLE

In order to cultivate faith in our homes, we parents must first and foremost come to know and love God and the Church ourselves. This means prioritizing prayer on a daily basis, being immersed in the sacred words of Scripture, receiving the Eucharist as frequently as possible, and seeing the face of Jesus Christ in those we serve both in our homes and in the world around us. Only when we are fully attuned to God will we be able to pass along our faith to our children. For busy parents, this often means letting our children "catch us" in the act of being people of faith.

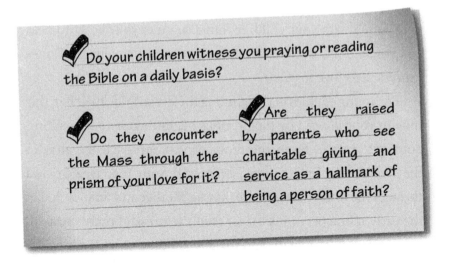

✔ Do your children witness you praying or reading the Bible on a daily basis?

✔ Do they encounter the Mass through the prism of your love for it?

✔ Are they raised by parents who see charitable giving and service as a hallmark of being a person of faith?

Many say that faith is "caught and not taught." In truth, a strong faith life probably stems equally from a vibrant education in the teachings of the Church and from learned behaviors modeled both formally and informally for our children. For families without a long track record of religious involvement, there can be great joy in taking baby steps together to grow in knowledge and commitment.

PRAY TOGETHER

If prayer has not been a large part of your life, join your children in adding regular prayer moments to your family's days together. Gather over breakfast or on the way to school for a brief morning offering. Bless your meals and the hands that have grown, prepared, and served it to you each time you dine. End your busy days with quiet bedtime prayers that recall the day and seek God's protection through the night. Learn the formal prayers of the Church with your children, but also quiet your heart to hear and emulate the simple, childlike ways in which your little ones express their love for God.

For young couples just beginning their family life together, this time in your life can be the precious beginning of your beautiful domestic church. From the moment you approach the altar in the sacrament of matrimony, consecrate your marriage to God through the intercession of the Blessed Mother and St. Joseph. Let the early moments of marriage, even the stressful ones, create in you a reflex to pray with and for one another. Open your hearts and home fully to the gift of life. Begin your own unique family traditions, not turning your backs on your families of origin but always remembering that your marriage and the new family you are creating come first.

"OPEN YOUR HEARTS AND HOME FULLY TO THE GIFT OF LIFE. BEGIN YOUR OWN UNIQUE FAMILY TRADITIONS."

BE ACTIVE

In order for faith to be cultivated in the home, it's also critical that our families have a second "home" in our parishes. Once you find a church home to worship in, make a firm commitment. Register as a member of the parish, but don't stop at just attending Mass on Sunday and dropping an envelope in the weekly collection. Just in the same way that you are a contributing member of your family, look for ways to more fully give of yourself and your gifts to your church home. Volunteer for a ministry. If you see something lacking at the parish, find a way to be a part of the solution. Meet and develop a relationship with the pastor at your church and any religious or clergy in the parish. Now, more than ever, our priests need our prayerful support for the challenging service they so lovingly render. Begin to see your parish as a second home by always looking for ways to give, to love, and to serve. In doing so, you lend to the creation of the environment we all want in our parish communities.

"ALWAYS BE LOOKING FOR WAYS TO GIVE, TO LOVE, AND TO SERVE."

BRINGING THE LITURGICAL CALENDAR TO LIFE

One of the most beautiful ways to live out the faith in our homes is to embrace the beauty of the Church's liturgical calendar. In the same way that many family traditions are built around holidays such as Christmas and Thanksgiving, Catholic celebrations can become the hallmark of our domestic churches. I'm not recommending expensive gifts, complicated crafts, or elaborate feasts for these commemorations. In fact, sometimes we can get so lost in the details of planning for a celebration that we lose sight of the cause for our joy.

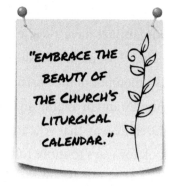

"EMBRACE THE BEAUTY OF THE CHURCH'S LITURGICAL CALENDAR."

All year long, our Catholic Church invites us into a deep relationship with one another. We recognize and live out together the liturgical seasons of Advent and Lent, with their complementary feasting seasons of Christmas and Easter. But we are also called to count together the days and weeks of Ordinary Time with their memorials, feast days, and solemnities. Indeed, in our Church every Sunday is a cause for celebration. In fact, almost every week marks the celebration of the life of a canonized saint or two. These feast days invite us into a deeper consideration of the lives of the holy men and women who have gone before us. They offer us very real role models of courage and sanctity for the challenges we face in our own lives. The saints become our friends and intercessors, carrying our heartfelt prayers to a God who loves us greatly. Teach your children to know and love the saints who are significant to your family. Choose a few that will be special to you in your own walk. Learn the details of their lives. Pray regularly through their intercession. Invoke their protection for your loved ones.

There are many beautiful and simple ways to live out the liturgical calendar in your home.

★ Begin the new liturgical year intentionally by placing an Advent wreath at the center of your family dinner table. As a part of your family's dinner hour, spend a few moments in quiet prayer around the wreath each day.

★ In anticipation of the season of Christmas, connect your family's giving to the true cause for the season. Consider simple gifts with religious significance or a gift to a charitable organization to avoid falling into the popular consumerism that has become so prevalent at Christmas. When our children were young, each boy received three gifts as we taught them to unite the cause for our celebration with the gifts of the wise men to the Christ Child in celebration of his birth.

★ Even young children can understand marking the season of Lent with the three devotions of prayer, fasting, and almsgiving. Although young ones are not called to the rules of fasting and abstinence, helping a young child to discern a "fast" from something simple like a new toy or a treat in order to prayerfully give a gift to someone in need can help them understand this time of prayerful penitence in anticipation of Easter.

★ Discuss with your children your own Lenten practices to help them see how your own season is helping you to draw into closer communion with Jesus Christ.

WITNESS AS A FAMILY

As you begin to more fully live out the liturgical calendar by celebrating family members' feast days or observing holy days throughout the year, you will find your domestic church beginning to thrive. Don't be afraid to try new traditions or to do things a little bit differently than what everyone else is doing in their homes. Being a family of faith sometimes means swimming against the tide of popular culture. When our friends and extended families begin to question why we celebrate things a bit differently in our homes, it offers us a beautiful opportunity to witness to the impact that living a life of faith can truly offer.

> "DON'T BE AFRAID TO TRY NEW TRADITIONS OR TO DO THINGS A LITTLE BIT DIFFERENTLY THAN WHAT EVERYONE ELSE IS DOING IN THEIR HOMES."

LISA M. HENDEY is the founder of CatholicMom.com and author of *The Grace of Yes* and the *Chime Travelers* series of books for children. She employs television, radio, social media, and her writing to share her passion for the New Evangelization and in support of the domestic church around the world. Lisa speaks internationally on faith, family, and technology and resides in the Diocese of Fresno with her husband, Greg.

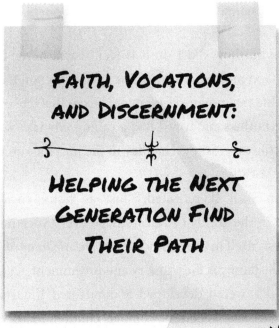

FAITH, VOCATIONS, AND DISCERNMENT:

HELPING THE NEXT GENERATION FIND THEIR PATH

FR. ANDREW CARL WISDOM, OP

WHAT ROLE DOES THE FAMILY PLAY IN FORMING VOCATIONS?

One winter morning when I was nine years old, I woke up with my left ear so swollen I couldn't get a knit cap over it. My mother rushed me to the hospital. That day, doctors saved my life from a massive infection in danger of spreading to my brain. A month later, I was again rushed into the operating room after the discovery that the infection had not been completely destroyed. My life had been saved a second time. Even as a child I knew the unlikely odds of that! "Mom, I understand how you can cheat death once, but how did I do it twice?" I will never forget her response, "God must have something special for you to do, some mission in life that no one else can do." From that day on, I never saw my life in the same way. I had a calling. My task was to find out its specific expression. That day in the hospital room was the birth of my vocation.

St. John Paul II reflected, "Just as Jesus' vocation was manifested in the family of Nazareth, so every vocation is born and manifests itself in the family" (from *The Meaning of Vocation*, Scepter). The family is the primary and preeminent place where a vocation is discovered, developed, and nurtured. It starts with the faith of the parents. When life compels children to ask questions like my own and others like it: "Why am I alive?" "How did I get here?" "Where am I going?" "What does life ultimately mean?" parents need to seize these teachable moments to share their faith.

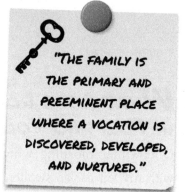

"THE FAMILY IS THE PRIMARY AND PREEMINENT PLACE WHERE A VOCATION IS DISCOVERED, DEVELOPED, AND NURTURED."

To be credible transmitters of the faith, you have to exemplify a two-fold authentic witness of Christian beliefs: a conscious, inward orientation toward love of God, and outward actions of loving service to others. Without these two elements, Christian witness is not present or fully alive. Focusing on the love of God by consistently praying at meals and before bed is natural with young children, but it's easy to overlook teaching service to others until later in the child's faith development.

The Catholic teaching of the Spiritual and Corporal Works of Mercy offer a user-friendly guide from which to begin your children's spiritual training. Witnessing to these works of mercy in your own life is foundational in your role as Christian parents.

Children are always watching what adults do. I'll never forget the first time I saw my mother kneeling by her bed in prayer or my father with tears in his eyes after receiving the Eucharist. There is never a moment your child is not looking to you as their primary example. Therefore, it is crucial to be intentional in the formation of your children's spiritual lives, "paying constant attention to the privileged relationship that [your] children have with their Father in heaven" (*The Meaning of Vocation*). I would add not only the privileged relationship with the Father but also their friendship with Jesus and Mary, and the Holy Spirit as a constant companion and guide. Children understand the importance of relationships, especially family relationships. So employ a relationship-based approach early on when transmitting your faith to your child. This introduces the central figures of the Scriptures as extended family members.

Family recitation of the rosary provides an excellent opportunity to build this relationship-based model with its spotlight on Jesus, Mary, and the guidance of the Holy Spirit in helping them carry out their unique role in the Father's plan for our salvation. Teaching your children to pray just one decade of the rosary on their own before bed is another way of introducing them to a lifelong habit of prayer based on the gift of relationship.

In a study conducted in 2005 by Vern Bengston, he found that "the parent-child faith transmission rate was 47 percent when the [parent's] relationship was close, but only 33 percent when it was not close" (*The CARA Report*). The strength of a marriage has other ramifications on child-rearing as well. The *Catechism* makes the point that the marriage sacrament blesses parents with the grace to "receive the responsibility and privilege of evangelizing their children" (CCC 2225). Being "evangelizers" to your children is probably not the first way you would define your role. But the *Catechism* is emphatic that parents "should initiate their children at an early age into the mysteries of the faith of which they are the 'first heralds' for their children. They should associate them from their tenderest years with the life of the Church" (CCC 2225). We see a similar emphasis in the rite of baptism when a child is initiated for the first time into the life of the Church as a full-fledged member of the body of Christ. Parents are called to be "the first teachers in the ways of the faith." Practically, teaching "the ways of faith" begins with teaching what it means to be Christian, to be Catholic, and the purpose of gathering each weekend to celebrate Eucharist together.

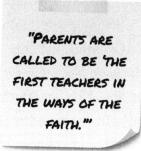

"PARENTS ARE CALLED TO BE 'THE FIRST TEACHERS IN THE WAYS OF THE FAITH.'"

As followers of Jesus, we are all sent forth at the end of every Mass to be evangelizers. The celebrant says in these or similar words, "Go in peace, glorifying the Lord with your lives," or "Go and announce the Good News." It's a reminder of the challenge Jesus gave us that we hear again and again in Mark 16:15, "Go into the whole world and proclaim the gospel to every creature." For the Christian, being an evangelizer is as natural as breathing. It's in our spiritual DNA. Pope Paul IV said: "Evangelizing is…the grace and vocation proper to the Church, her deepest identity. She exists in order to evangelize" (*Evangelii Nuntiandi*, 14). We are the Church. Evangelizing is our deepest identity. It's our central mission in life. It's why we exist. Should not our children be the primary recipients of this great missionary call of ours? After all, they will be called to do the same some day.

"WE ARE THE CHURCH. EVANGELIZING IS OUR DEEPEST IDENTITY."

EVANGELIZE YOUR CHILDREN

So what is evangelization?

Before every football game, former NFL quarterback Tim Tebow would not only apply eye black around his eyes to keep out the glare like other players, but would write John 3:16 in white on top. Not only does that passage carry the essence of good news that is the substance of our evangelization, but that very act at each and every game is an example of evangelization. While many were edified by Tebow's gesture, others ridiculed him. Yet, he never stopped publicly witnessing to his faith. Where do we invite our children to publicly witness to their faith? Unwittingly, we may teach the opposite, that it is somehow unseemly to express our faith publicly or that it is rude to, as the old saying goes, "wear your religion on your sleeve."

Angela Bursch, a Catholic mother of five children ranging from seven to eighteen years of age, notes that her children's witness to their faith "can be done in a myriad of ways. For one child, it is quiet one-on-one discussion while riding the school bus about what the beads she is holding are for. For another, it is defending the faith during a class discussion. For another, it is the quiet witness of faith in how he treats other people, especially his siblings." Angela gratefully concludes, "There is nothing more beautiful to me than to hear our children pray spontaneously from the heart." The goal of all Catholic communities (not just parents) is to

"THE GOAL OF ALL CATHOLIC COMMUNITIES IS TO RAISE KIDS AS DISCIPLES."

raise kids as disciples, those who become the intimate friends of Jesus because of their living encounter with him as an infinite love that embraces them.

HOW CAN THE FAMILY FOSTER VOCATIONS?

According to the *Catechism*, parents "have the mission of teaching their children to pray and to discover their vocation as children of God" (*CCC* 2226). It follows then that instead of asking your children the proverbial question, "What do you want to do when you grow up?" we need to ask, "What do you think God is calling you to do with your life when you grow up?" The focus shifts from what I want to what God wants and introduces the young person early in life to the bedrock Christian principle that our lives are not our own. "Whether we live or die, we are the Lord's," St. Paul says (Romans 14:8). Fostering vocations begins first with the language we use, the vocabulary we introduce, and the questions we ask. Do they reflect our faith that God is the source and summit of our lives?

As we delve deeper into the issue of fostering vocations, we should clarify what the term means. If you asked someone on the street what a vocation is, he might immediately associate it with a particular technical skill learned from a vocational school, say for automotive skills or electronics. The other most common association with the word *vocation* is someone called to be a priest or a religious whether a cloistered nun, active sister, or lay brother.

Vocation comes from the Latin word *vocare*, which means "to call." As the Second Vatican Council made clear, each of us, by virtue of our baptism into the Christian family, receives a call to holiness. In the Dogmatic Constitution on the Church (*Lumen Gentium*), Vatican II's inspirational document on the mystery of the Church, we learn that God chose to raise up men and women of every age to share in his divine life and to be formed through our baptism into the likeness of his Son. "Through Baptism and Confirmation all are appointed to this apostolate by the Lord himself....The laity, however, are given this special vocation: to make the Church present and fruitful in those places and circumstances where it is only through them that she can become the salt of the earth. Thus, every lay person, through those gifts given to him, is at once the witness and the living instrument of the mission of the Church itself" (*LG* 28:4). This is the deepest meaning of our baptismal vocation: the call to actively journey in holiness with Christ and the Church. That vocation is fulfilled in a specific way and we trust God to reveal it.

To discover our vocation we need help, primarily from our biological and parish family, to look for the signs of how God thinks it best we live that call (as an intentionally single lay person, married, religious, or ordained). This requires families to encourage a trust and willingness on the part of their children to be open and generous to their unique call from God. Religious life and priesthood reflect a less common, more particular call from God.

> "EACH OF US, BY VIRTUE OF OUR BAPTISM INTO THE CHRISTIAN FAMILY, RECEIVES A CALL TO HOLINESS."

START A CONVERSATION ABOUT THE CALL?

Children are inquisitive. They are around married people and single adults often. What is not so common is exposure to those living the priesthood or religious life. Our parishes are much larger than they used to be, and there are fewer priests and religious whom children can get to know. So when children ask about these vocations, take them seriously! Invite a priest, brother, or sister to dinner. Encourage your child to follow up with your guest by written note, email, or a phone call and develop a personal rapport.

Get the whole family involved in your parish by serving Mass, being lectors or eucharistic ministers, working in the parish pantry or soup kitchen, or teaching CCD. Introduce the practice of spiritual reading to your

> "WHEN CHILDREN ASK ABOUT THESE VOCATIONS, TAKE THEM SERIOUSLY."

child whether on a saint's life or a chapter of the Scriptures each night. The earlier the better! History shows that religious and priestly vocations awaken early but are often not nurtured and encouraged in a consistent way. As a family, share your day during your evening meal in the light of faith. Encourage conversations about discernment and living your vocation.

You may also need to address some fear-based myths about the religious or priestly vocations and debunk them in a way your children can understand. Below are four of the most common.

I will be lonely: Every life has moments of true loneliness, even those who are married with children. Priests do, too. But in study after study, priests report that they are happy. In fact, they have one of the highest rates of happiness among professions!

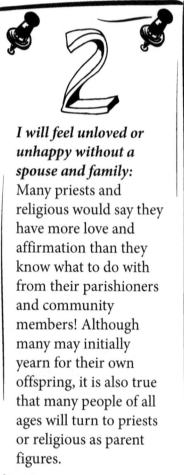

I will feel unloved or unhappy without a spouse and family: Many priests and religious would say they have more love and affirmation than they know what to do with from their parishioners and community members! Although many may initially yearn for their own offspring, it is also true that many people of all ages will turn to priests or religious as parent figures.

I'm not sure I can live without being with a woman or a man sexually: Although we are wired as human beings to be sexual and to procreate, we can live without genital expression. What we can't live without is intimacy. Think of it this way. If sexuality were an airport, there would be a lot of different gates from which to choose. Genital expression is only one of those gates. Generativity, creativity, and intimacy are other gates and in some ways more indispensable as expressions of your sexuality than sex is by itself. They touch upon the very core of the soul.

I have to give up my independence: Broadly speaking, yes you do. When you make promises to your bishop or profess vows to a religious superior, you give your life away to God for service in a diocese or religious order. Married couples also relinquish their independence to one another. The way a priest or religious gives up freedom is different, but paradoxically, there is a whole new gift in being freed from the preoccupations that accompany life "in the world" such as career, livelihood, and the responsibility of raising children. You are free to be totally available to God in the specific work he wants you to do through the decisions of your bishop or religious superior.

WHEN TO START TALKING ABOUT DISCERNMENT?

The *Catechism* instructs that education in the faith "should begin in the child's earliest years" (*CCC* 2226). But how do we do that? Luckily the *Catechism* gives us an answer, too, when "family members help one another to grow in faith by the witness of a Christian life in keeping with the Gospel. Family catechesis precedes, accompanies, and enriches other forms of instruction in the faith" (*CCC* 2226). This is true whether you are homeschooling, sending your children to Catholic schools, or enrolling them in the public schools. At the heart of family faith formation is introducing the young person to the critical discipline of discernment early in life.

> "AT THE HEART OF FAMILY FAITH FORMATION IS INTRODUCING THE YOUNG PERSON TO THE CRITICAL DISCIPLINE OF DISCERNMENT."

What do we mean by discernment? "Discernment is the process whereby we discover God's presence and action in our lives. Before making a decision, we intentionally stop to consider and reflect upon how our desires match with what God wants for us. The goal of discernment is to discover God's personal and wholly unique call to us, to me" (*Tuning In To God's Call*). The ancient spiritual writer John Climacus, in *The Ladder of Divine Ascent*, defined discernment as "a solid understanding of the will of God in all times, in all places, in all things; and it is found among those who are pure in heart, in body and in speech." Discernment is ultimately about each of us becoming free to become in heart, body, and speech, the person God made us to be, the person God wants us to be. We are always after a truer answer to the perennial question: Who am I as a child of God?

As a pilgrim people on a journey together, our relationship with others as Catholics is a solid starting point for discernment. There are no solo fights to sanctity! That is never truer than in our family, the foundation of all our other communities in which our discernment of God's will and our unique calling continue to unfold. Understanding our calling and acting on it in integrity is a lifelong process. In the meantime, as parents, focus your child first on the God who calls and second, on the path he should choose. Most of all, teach children not to be afraid to get it wrong.

With regard to a specific vocational expression, Catholics traditionally ask themselves, "Should my life commitment be to sacramental marriage, the intentional single life, religious life, or priesthood? As we stated earlier, the word *vocation*, from its Latin roots, means "call" or "voice." Before you can pursue a vocation, you have to hear that "still small voice" calling within. Whether priestly or religious life, married, or an intentional single life, we have to wrestle with discerning an authentic Christian vocational choice. We need to teach our children the discipline of discernment early on if they are to successfully and courageously discover their own vocations.

Vocational discernment is not something weird or unusual. We all have to do it throughout our lives. Parents have an opportunity—and a duty—to begin the process with their children, showing them the rich and graced possibilities of the

Spirit's call in their lives! If you're still not sure where to start, here are some questions you can reflect on as a family.

"VOCATIONAL DISCERNMENT IS NOT WEIRD OR UNUSUAL. WE ALL HAVE TO DO IT."

Why Discern? The impetus for our discernment is to continue what began at our baptism when we were claimed for Christ and committed our lives to God. Our first step is to intentionally seek to discover the unique design that God has drawn for our life.

What to Discern? The Church invites us to give a generous gift of our self to God through either married life, an intentional single life, priesthood, or religious life. God wants us not merely to survive in our life choices but to flourish. We discern where the Holy Spirit is telling us we will truly flourish.

Where Do I Begin Discerning? We begin discerning right in the landscape of our own lives and daily communities of family and friends; in the events, encounters, and efforts of our everyday experiences. We learn to recognize our various gifts, talents, and desires as the seeds planted in the soil of our lives as signs of our vocation.

How Does Discernment Lead to Decision? Discernment is both an interior and an exterior exercise. Interiorly, we pray daily, meditate on Scripture or a spiritual book, and seek God's voice within. Exteriorly, we seek the advice of others, exploring the various vocational choices through spiritual direction, Come & See vocation weekends, and retreats. We wrestle openly with our fears, doubts, or concerns. Then we make a decision knowing that faith is not a certainty because of what is clearly seen, but the convicted assurance of the unseen things for which we hope.

What are the Signs of a Good Discernment? Do you have increased clarity in your discernment? Strong intuition? Do you have peace once you've made your decision? Peace does not mean the absence of some concern in taking that leap of faith we are called to make with a particular path, but that we have a calm sense of God's presence in the decision.

FR. ANDREW CARL WISDOM, OP, is a Dominican priest and preacher. He has more than a decade of experience in vocations ministry and currently serves as vicar for mission advancement and director of the Society for Vocational Support for the Dominicans, Province of St. Albert the Great. Fr. Wisdom authored *Tuning In to God's Call* and *Why I Should Encourage My Son to Be a Priest* (both Liguori, 2012.)

Church, the Home, and Putting It Together:

Building Up Your Domestic Church

Donna-Marie Cooper O'Boyle

<u>Your</u> Church

The Catholic presence stretches around the globe and its numbers are increasing worldwide, according to Vatican statistics. About 1.2 billion baptized Catholics belong to the "big" Church, the body of Christ. This doesn't include about 4.8 million Catholics not taken into account because they are located in countries (mainly China and North Korea) that could not provide accurate counts to the Vatican. In many cases, Catholics are not only a part of the universal Church but are also living in one of the countless little domestic churches throughout the world.

But what actually constitutes a domestic church? Let's take a quick look at the beginning of our Church founder's life. Jesus was born into the heart of a family, a little domestic church consisting of his mother, Mary, his foster father, St. Joseph, and himself. Wherever the Holy Family set up their home—in the stable in Bethlehem, in Egypt, or in Nazareth—their domestic church moved along with them simply because their domestic church consisted of the three of them—their family.

Through the ages, as people were converted and became believers, "they desired that 'their whole household' should also be saved. These families who became believers were islands of Christian life in an unbelieving world" (CCC 1655).

Every Christian family in essence should possess a missionary spirit and is called by God to proclaim the Gospel. Just as early Christian families were excellent examples to those around them, Catholic families today can build up their own domestic churches and strive to be "islands of Christian life in an unbelieving world." Our Church encourages us. Specifically, Pope Paul VI when speaking about evangelization, explained in his apostolic exhortation *Evangelii Nuntiandi*, "At different moments in the Church's history and also in the Second Vatican Council, the family has well deserved the beautiful name of 'domestic church.' This means that there should be found in every Christian family the various aspects of the entire Church.

Every home is called to become a domestic church.

Furthermore, the family, like the Church, ought to be a place where the Gospel is transmitted and from which the Gospel radiates" (*EN* 71).

Pope Benedict XVI said, "[E]very home can transform itself into a little church. Not only in the sense that in them must reign the typical Christian love made of altruism and of reciprocal care, but still more in the sense that the whole of family life, based on faith, is called to revolve around the singular lordship of Jesus Christ."

Although these are wonderful ideals to emulate, we know that today not every Catholic family consists of a mother and a father. A large number of domestic churches are run by a single parent because of a child born out of wedlock, separation or divorce, or a spouse's passing. Broken and nontraditional families seem more the norm than the exception. Grandparents are raising their grandchildren in many households. And even in "traditional" families, not every Catholic husband and wife mirrors the mystery of Christ's love for the Church, his bride. No matter what our family looks like, our Church summons Catholic families to live in this virtuous way. Each unique domestic church can be a stable, loving, and holy environment.

> "CATHOLIC FAMILIES TODAY CAN BE ISLANDS OF CHRISTIAN LIFE IN AN UNBELIEVING WORLD."

While navigating everyday household busyness, especially during challenges, we might forget that we reside in a "domestic church." But God will grant families the graces they need to strive

"EACH UNIQUE DOMESTIC CHURCH CAN BE A STABLE, LOVING, AND HOLY ENVIRONMENT."

for holiness in the family as they navigate the stresses, strains, and indescribable joys of every day.

The domestic church begins with the sacrament of matrimony—man and woman become husband and wife. Saint John Paul II spoke of a Catholic couple's call to holiness within that sacrament when he said in *Love and Responsibility*, "Marriage is an act of will that signifies and involves a mutual gift, which unites the spouses and binds them to their eventual souls, with whom they make up a sole family—a domestic church."

He goes on to explain the husband and wife's responsibility to recognize and to act upon their role as "givers of life" in his encyclical *Evangelium Vitae* (The Gospel of Life):

> As the domestic church, the family is summoned to proclaim, celebrate, and serve the gospel of life....In giving origin to a new life, parents recognize that the child "as the fruit of their mutual gift of love, is in turn, a gift for both of them, a gift flows from them" (*EV* 92).

As babies are born and families grow, the parents, considered the first and foremost educators by the Church, are called to pass on the Catholic faith to their children. Blessed Mother Teresa explained this experience in the domestic church very simply, "The best and surest way to learn the love of Jesus is through the family." Single-parent households are also called by God to pass on the faith. Time should be set aside so that children can learn their faith lessons. As well, the virtues that are naturally practiced in daily living will greatly impact the growing children. Every Christian home can be an abode of love and prayer.

"GOD WILL GRANT YOU THE GRACE YOU NEED TO NAVIGATE THE STRESS, STRAIN, AND JOY OF EVERYDAY LIFE."

CURRICULUM OF LOVE AND FORGIVENESS

The Church tells us, "The family finds in the plan of God the Creator and Redeemer not only its identity, what it is, but also its mission, what it can and should do....Each family finds within itself a summons that cannot be ignored, and that specifies both its dignity and its responsibility: family, become what you are" (*Familiaris Consortio*, 17).

Catholic parents can look to the *Catechism* for direction regarding their responsibilities to pass on the faith to their children. There we learn, "The Christian home is the place where children receive the first proclamation of the faith. For this reason the family home is rightly called 'the domestic church,' a community of grace and prayer, a school of human virtues and of Christian charity" (*CCC* 1666). Within the walls of the domestic church, children will learn about their faith through their parent's and grandparent's word and example, as well as within the many growing pains and nitty-gritty details of everyday life as a family grows together in holiness.

Sometimes life in the family looks like anything but a page out of the *Catechism*. Pope Francis unambiguously stated, "There are always arguments in marriages, and at times even plates are thrown." But, thankfully, "Love is stronger than the moments in which we argue." He encouraged married couples "never to let the day draw to an end without making peace…Married life is beautiful," he said, "and must be protected." Everyday life in the family may seem filled with a lot of ordinariness and at times a little (or a lot!) of chaos. Yet, right there along with the normal routines and day-to-day occurrences of sibling rivalry, teenage angst, and grouchy spouses is woven a paradigm of human enrichment pointing us to a narrow path that leads to heaven.

Catholic teachings open our eyes to the remarkable goings on within a growing faithful Catholic family, helping us to recognize that there is a heck of a lot more happening in our day-to-day lives than what meets the eye! "It is here that the father of the family, the mother, children, and all members of the family exercise the priesthood of the baptized in a privileged way 'by the reception of the sacraments, prayer and thanksgiving, the witness of a holy life, and self-denial and active charity.' Thus the home is the first school of Christian life and 'a school for human enrichment.' Here one learns

> "ALONG WITH THE NORMAL ROUTINES AND DAY-TO-DAY OCCURRENCES OF SIBLING RIVALRY, TEENAGE ANGST, AND GROUCHY SPOUSES IS WOVEN A PARADIGM OF HUMAN ENRICHMENT POINTING US TO A NARROW PATH THAT LEADS TO HEAVEN."

endurance and the joy of work, fraternal love, generous—even repeated—forgiveness, and above all divine worship in prayer and the offering of one's life" (*CCC* 1657).

Amazing! And we might have thought we were simply teaching our kids how to share, love, pray, potty train, break up fights, function as lovingly as possible after sleepless nights, lay down the law, and rescue them from too many lurking dangers. But, in reality, it is within the domestic church that we Catholic parents lay out a curriculum of fraternal love and forgiveness, through practicing the virtues, even heroic ones, while helping our family to work out our salvation in the give-and-take of life in the family.

BUILDING THE DOMESTIC CHURCH

Whether we live in a palace, a bungalow, or a cave, Catholic parents have the awesome responsibility of raising their children to not only learn right from wrong but also to recognize that the real purpose of their lives in this world is to work out their salvation for the next world—their eternal lives. This has to be the top priority when raising Christian children. God provides the blessing of a family structure to accomplish this.

As first and foremost educator, parents will ultimately be answering to God with regard to how their children have been educated. That means parents need to investigate all that is going on in their children's education, not only at home but also in their schools, both Catholic and public, and their religious-education programs.

There can be no doubt that there is a tremendous amount of work that needs to be carried out on a regular basis within the heart of the home. In addition to the constant vigilant care of growing children, there is the never-ending housework too. I love what Blessed Mother Teresa expressed: "It is not how much we do that is pleasing to God, but how much love we put into the doing" (*Love: A Fruit Always in Season*). There will never be a shortage of tasks to complete in a domestic church, but parents are wise to try to remember this saintly woman's inspired sentiment. We should endeavor to put a big measure of love into all that we do and not simply go through the motions in order to check off a "to-do" list.

Parents in a traditional dual-parent household can work together to form a united front in raising their children and caring for the household. It is beneficial for children to observe and feel reassured that both of their parents care about their well-being and work together as the heads of the household to bring harmony to their domestic church. Any disagreements are preferably discussed in private.

Catholic single parents may feel very alone at times because we still live in a couple's world. Caring for the children without a spouse can be strenuous and at times overwhelming. Tiptoeing in and out of Mass with noisy youngsters is difficult when you have other little ones and no one to assist you. This fact alone can inhibit some single parents from going to church. Imagine how this scene would change if other Catholics pitched in to be of assistance!

In mixed-faith households, passing on the faith to the children can be challenging. Being married to a non-Catholic or a non-believer can sometimes feel as if you are a single parent because you are shouldering the job of conveying the faith alone. In that case, parents should try their very best to teach their children the faith and get involved with any available programs that can be helpful. God is certainly aware of this plight and will grant many graces in this area.

Despite the challenges for single-parent, mixed-faith, or mixed-believing households, through practicing virtues of faith, hope, and love these parents can indeed build beautiful domestic churches where their children will thrive and blossom in the Catholic faith.

EYES TOWARD HEAVEN

To help pave the way to heaven for our children, it's essential for us as parents to establish an atmosphere of prayer in our home. We first need to ground ourselves in prayer, making it an integral part of our daily lives. Getting on our knees first thing in the morning and offering our day to the Lord gets us headed in the right direction.

If children are raised in a household of prayer, prayer will become as natural as breathing and will provide a secure foundation. Kids take cues from their best role models, their parents and grandparents. The example of prayers said in the morning and evening, for special intentions at various times, and at the dinner table speaks volumes because children look to adults and learn their behaviors.

To help our family focus more on the sacred than the secular, we must bring something of the big Church into our little domestic church. We do that by placing sacred images around our home. Sacred art, icons, crucifixes, images of the Sacred Heart of Jesus, the Immaculate Heart of Mary, the Holy Family, pictures of saints, sacramentals, holy water fonts, and even a prayer corner can adorn our homes. These holy items help stir the soul and lift our attention toward heaven and its rewards. We will also be establishing faith traditions in our children's lives that they will hopefully carry into their future domestic churches.

"GETTING ON OUR KNEES FIRST THING IN THE MORNING AND OFFERING OUR DAY TO THE LORD GETS US HEADED IN THE RIGHT DIRECTION."

PRAYING IN THE DOMESTIC CHURCH

Simply put, "A family that prays together stays together," said Fr. Patrick Peyton, CSC. Additionally, our *Catechism* tells us, "the Christian family is the first place for education in prayer" (CCC 2694). We must endeavor to lay down a foundation of prayer in our domestic churches. It will undoubtedly be one of the most important things we will ever do as Christian parents and grandparents, godparents, aunts, and uncles.

Prayer comes from the depths of our hearts and stretches up like incense to reach God. It is through the gift of faith that we pray. The Holy Spirit teaches the faithful to pray in hope. We learn from the psalms, "I wait for the LORD; who bends down to me and hears my cry" (Psalms 40:2). Love is at the very core of prayer. So, we see that the theological virtues of faith, hope, and love are tightly woven together in the mystery of prayer. To hand down the amazing gift of prayer to the family, we can start with our own example of praying in the company of our family, showing them that we can offer up prayers at any time, whether there is a particular need or just a desire to thank God for his many blessings.

We should also try to establish specific times to pray together as a family, such as morning and evening prayers, a family rosary (or even just a decade), and grace before and after meals. A gentle approach to teaching prayer is preferred over a strict regimented one. We want to impress upon our children that prayer is, in reality, a personal conversation with God.

Setting up a prayer table or prayer corner provides a tangible way for the family to focus on prayer. And throughout the daily give-and-take within the family, dealing with inconveniences, differences, and occasional discord, the family learns the valuable lesson of offering it all to God right in the details of ordinary life, helping one another get to heaven.

SETTING UP YOUR PRAYER CORNER

As noted, a few sacred tangible items placed in view makes praying more touchable for our kids. A prayer table or prayer corner set up in a gathering area of the home can help to draw our attention to the sacred rather than the secular.

To create this prayer corner, simply place a small table somewhere in your house that best suits your needs. A beautiful icon or a crucifix can be hung on the wall above the table. A Bible, prayer books, holy water, and basket of rosary beads can be placed on the table. Children's saint's books and Bible stories can fill a basket or bookshelf nearby. You might want your prayer table to reflect the various seasons in the liturgical year, adorning it with flowers on holy

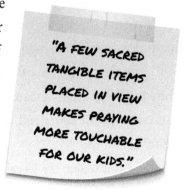

"A FEW SACRED TANGIBLE ITEMS PLACED IN VIEW MAKES PRAYING MORE TOUCHABLE FOR OUR KIDS."

days or Marian feast days. A candle can be lit or incense burned (with adult supervision) for family prayers, making the occasion of prayer more ceremonious.

Children can sit on pillows or mats as they gather for morning or evening prayer or while listening to an age-appropriate inspirational story. They can be encouraged to draw holy pictures to decorate the area. Prayer petitions can be scribbled on paper and placed on the prayer table.

This unique area will grow with your children as you replace the large wooden rosary beads with grown-up beads and swap out the little kid books for more mature ones. With a little time, some thought, and prayer, you will have fashioned a little oratory for holy encounters, a place of refuge. Even when not in use, your prayer corner stands as a reminder of a holy reason for your days within the home.

NOURISHING BODIES AND SOULS

Dinnertime is a lot more than just about filling our bellies. I am convinced that amazing things happen when families gather to reconnect at the end of the day to break bread at the family table. Dinnertime is a distinctive time to grow together as a family, creating memories and establishing traditions.

Our dinner conversations may not always be so profound and our children's behavior may not always be Hallmark picture- perfect (many times far from it!). Things happen, kids can get messy and loud, and we may lose our patience at times. We are human, after all. Everything in the home is a work in progress, and parents are wise to lower expectations with regard to their children's behavior while still teaching them to show respect and practice their manners as best they can. Meal times are certainly those occasions when "tenderness, forgiveness, respect, fidelity, and disinterested service are the rule." Let's be present to one another and be sure that no one (including parents) is using phones and devices at the dinner table.

Introducing prayer at the dinner table is not only beneficial, it's essential. Why not use the time wisely? You will have a captive audience, after all. After grace is said, you can add an Our Father and a Hail Mary and any special intentions. In just a few minutes' time, you will have united your family in prayer.

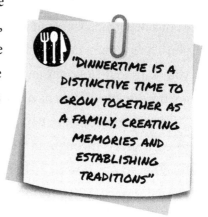

"DINNERTIME IS A DISTINCTIVE TIME TO GROW TOGETHER AS A FAMILY, CREATING MEMORIES AND ESTABLISHING TRADITIONS"

Although we know we should do our very best in teaching the faith to our children, remarkably our children also teach us! It's incredible to know that our children actually help us in our sanctification process. "Children in turn contribute to the growth in holiness of the parents" (*CCC* 2227). Where would we be without our children? That's a question we should ponder. They help to keep us on the straight and narrow!

TO THE ENDS OF THE EARTH!

The Christian family is "the first and vital cell of society" (*Familiaris Consortio*). Because the Christian husband and wife receive the divine gift of love from God through their sacramental marriage, they can live and communicate that love to their children within their domestic church and then offer it to the world. Saint John Paul II instructed, "The family has the mission to guard, reveal and communicate love" (*FC* 17). Christian families are called by God to not merely exist in their domestic churches but to go out of their households and love their fellow human beings within the fabric of society, offering peace, understanding, and perhaps a healing balm to our depersonalized and troubled world. Jesus instructed, "I give you a new commandment: love one another. As I have loved you, so you also should love one another. This is how all will know that you are my disciples, if you have love for one another" (John 13:34, 35).

God provides Christian families with countless opportunities to earn grace throughout our lives as we forge a blessed bond together in our homes, helping each other to come closer to our eternal reward. When we are out and about in the neighborhood and community, through each encounter, our families can become a powerful Christian influence, a vibrant beacon of light in our darkened world.

BUILDING YOUR DOMESTIC CHURCH

The following are easy, practical ways to build your own domestic church. You can try them all or just pick the ones that are the best fit for your families.

The Blessing of the Home: Whether your domestic church is a house or an apartment, invite a priest to come to bless it, either when you first move in or at any time while you are living there.

Enthronements: In addition to blessing your home, you may enthrone your home to the Sacred Heart of Jesus and the Immaculate Heart of Mary. Invite a priest to assist you with the enthronement or do it on your own by hanging up the images in your home and praying the following prayer together.

Act of Family Consecration

Most Sacred Heart of Jesus and Immaculate Heart of Mary, we consecrate ourselves and our entire family to you. We consecrate to you: our very being and all our life. All that we are. All that we have. And all that we love. To you we give our bodies, our hearts, and our souls. To you we dedicate our home and our country. Mindful of this consecration, we promise you to live the Christian way by the practice of Christian virtues, with great regard for respect for one another. O Most Sacred Heart of Jesus and Immaculate Heart of Mary, accept our humble confidence and this Act of Consecration by which we entrust ourselves and all our family to you. Most Sacred Heart of Jesus, have mercy on us. Immaculate Heart of Mary, pray for us.

Devotions: Praying the rosary is a popular devotion for many Catholic families, who, through its mysteries reflect on significant events in Scripture pertaining to Jesus and Mary. Wearing the brown scapular is a devotion whereby the person places himself or herself under the protection of the Blessed Mother. Wearing a blessed miraculous medal is another devotion connected to the Blessed Virgin Mary based on her messages to St. Catherine Laboure. The Blessed Mother said, "Have a medal struck upon this model. All those who wear it, when it is blessed, will receive great graces especially if they wear it round the neck."

Sacred images and sacramentals: A domestic church should be filled with sacred images and sacramentals. Holy pictures and crucifixes should be hung throughout. A holy water font can be placed by the front door in order to bless oneself with holy water and remind you of your baptism. Holy water should be regularly sprinkled throughout the home. Blessed salt can be used as well.

Parental Blessings: Parents can trace the sign of the cross with their thumb or forefinger on their child's forehead at any time while asking God to bless him or her.

Celebrate Name Days: Celebrate your family's name days, which are the days dedicated to each person's patron saint.

Celebrate Baptismal Days: Celebrate your children's (and your own) baptismal days by having a special dinner, dessert, praying special prayers, and thanking God for the gift of your baptism.

Follow the Liturgical Year: Families can pray the Liturgy of the Hours together.

Creating Family Traditions: Family traditions can be established. Dinnertime should be enjoyed together as a time for connecting as a family, sharing and praying together. Avoid too many evening activities that take you out of the home and disturb family dinnertime. You can incorporate a holy pilgrimage into the family vacation by visiting shrines.

PRAYERS

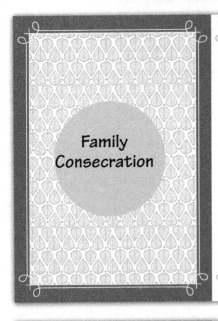

Family Consecration

Jesus, Mary, Joseph! Graciously accept our family, which we dedicate and consecrate to you. Be pleased to protect, guard, and keep it in sincere faith, in peace and in the harmony of Christian charity. By conforming ourselves to the divine model of your family, may we all attain eternal happiness. Amen.

Prayer for a Family

Lord, bless our family, all of us now together, those far away, all who are gone back to you. May we know joy. May we bear our sorrows in patience. Let love guide our understanding of each other. Let us be grateful to each other. We have all made each other what we are. O family of Jesus, watch over our family. Amen.

Morning Offering

O Jesus, through the Immaculate Heart of Mary, I offer you all my prayers, works, joys, and sufferings of this day, for all the intentions of your Scared Heart, in union with the holy sacrifice of the Mass throughout the world, in reparation for my sins, for the intentions of all my relatives and friends and in particular of the Holy Father. Amen.

Grace Before Meals

Bless us, O Lord, and these thy gifts which we are about to receive from thy bounty. Through Christ, our Lord. Amen.

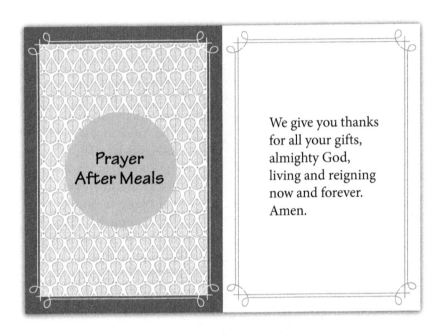

Prayer After Meals

We give you thanks for all your gifts, almighty God, living and reigning now and forever. Amen.

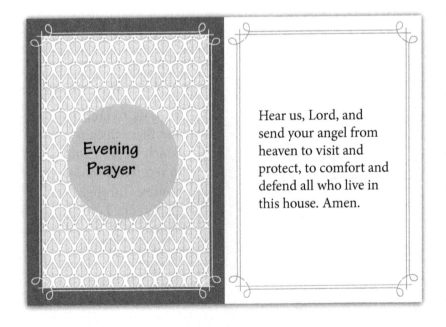

Evening Prayer

Hear us, Lord, and send your angel from heaven to visit and protect, to comfort and defend all who live in this house. Amen.

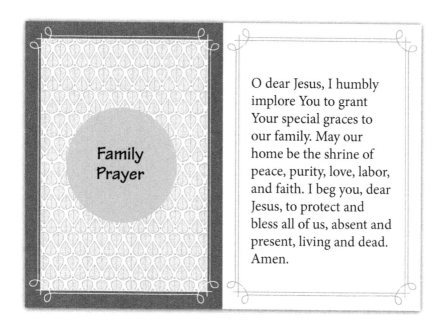

Family Prayer

O dear Jesus, I humbly implore You to grant Your special graces to our family. May our home be the shrine of peace, purity, love, labor, and faith. I beg you, dear Jesus, to protect and bless all of us, absent and present, living and dead. Amen.

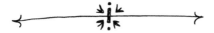

DONNA-MARIE COOPER O'BOYLE is a Catholic wife and mother of five on earth and three in heaven. She is an award-winning and best-selling journalist and author of twenty books, catechist, speaker, pilgrimage host, and the EWTN television host of *Everyday Blessings for Catholic Moms* and *Catholic Mom's Cafe,* which she created. Donna-Marie was blessed to know Fr. John A. Hardon, SJ, and Blessed Mother Teresa. You can find her at donnacooperoboyle.com and viewdomesticchurch.blogspot.com.

THE REAL WORLD
FEED THE CAT
MASS
CONFERENCE CALL @ 7:00 PM.
GYM?
RCIA CLASS
YOUTH GROUP MEETING
PICK UP KIDS

Family, Faith, and Everything Else:

Challenges Facing the 21st-Century Family

Donald J. Paglia

Navigating an Ocean of Anxiety

Family life is a sacred calling. It is a busy, relational, and messy but nevertheless, sacred life—one that is very different from a monastic life. Fr. Ronald Rolheiser, OMI, wrote that "God is more domestic than monastic." He quoted novelist Nikos Kazantzakis, who said, "God is more domestic than monastic." This vision of the sacred in the ordinary often gets missed or ignored. We view family life as only busy and merely hectic. Families are both messy and holy! Our Church often holds up ideals such as individual meditation and quiet shrines, of individual piety within an exclusive adult community, and orderliness. This conveys a message that the

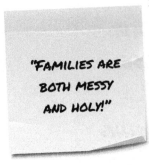

"FAMILIES ARE BOTH MESSY AND HOLY!"

messy and chaotic reality of adult-and-children family living is somehow a lesser spirituality. Monastic life is, of course, its own sacred calling for men and women religious. It is, however, not a calling for familied people. Christian families would do well to incorporate some slowing down and a bit of piety germane to monastics, but contemplative spirituality is not the mainstay for a family spirituality; nor should it be.

Today's families are bombarded by both exterior and interior dynamics that constantly overrun contemporary family life. Fans of *Star Trek: The Next Generation* fans may recall Captain Jean-Luc Picard of the USS Enterprise being captured by the Borg and told, "Resistance is futile." This is often how we feel about the countless distractions that find their way into our lives. Technology has contributed greatly to our lives, but it has also become embedded into our schools, our work places, and our homes, making our family life more complicated and more open to outside influence than it once might have been. Parents can feel overwhelmed and think there is no escape. In addition, today's parents are barraged with everything from peanut-butter allergies to political correctness, child safety, sexual exploitation, and much more, often fueled by media hype. We live in an unprecedented, perplexing, and overwhelming time that has parents stressing out as they overmanage, overschedule, or overprotect their children. Many children and their parents are swimming in an ocean of anxiety.

With all these outside anxieties, it is easy for the genuine love of parents to get displaced or buried as parents stress over the issues their children face, such as: schooling, health concerns, and safety. Caring can also be a disguise for anxiety, and too often dictates how and what parents do with and for their children. Parents today appear to be running at such a frenetic pace, often sleep-deprived, while they try to provide for their family. This leaves little or no time for their marital relationship, let alone for their own individual selves. Why wouldn't this be the case when the perception of the world is one of such massive uncertainty and danger? There seems to be a failure of vision; a vision for our world and of our place in it. Albert Einstein once asked if we see the universe as friendly. Most do not. This is disheartening when we also say we are Christians. For us there is a different experience of life, or at least a different one available to us who seek it. "I live, no longer I, but Christ lives in me," says St. Paul (Galatians 2:20). It is in our Christian family where we assist one another toward this Christ-centered way.

> "WE LIVE IN AN UNPRECEDENTED, PERPLEXING, AND OVERWHELMING TIME THAT HAS PARENTS STRESSING OUT AS THEY OVER-MANAGE, OVER-SCHEDULE, OR OVER-PROTECT THEIR CHILDREN."

THE FUTURE PASSES THROUGH THE FAMILY

The Roman Catholic Church tells us that the Christian family is the basic building block of society and that the Christian family has a mission. When it says this though, it is often done in ecclesial language—language that is difficult for laity to comprehend. The focus is often on what families are not doing, what isn't happening, or what is wrong. In some cases, it has been a message of going back to how life may have been lived in a past nostalgic version of family life. Today's families need and deserve more.

We need to speak in a familial language—one that embraces today's families' everyday, ordinary, realities. Familial spirituality needs to be held up as the valid and authentic sacredness of the domestic church—the church of the home.

Both single parents and married parents need tangible things like babysitting, home-based programming, and events at convenient times, as well as other creative ways to hear the Church's prophetic message for the Christian family. In other words, families need the local parish's assistance in carrying out the Christian family's mission. Support and inspiration must come from a place of humility and love, as well as one of a genuine partnership.

Our entire Church family needs to adopt new ways that consider the daily rhythms and realities of family life, while helping families incorporate realistic meditation, reflection, and prayerfulness into their lives as they draw upon and discern the will of the Creator. These practices should be integrated into the already present elements of family spirituality, which is lived out in the busy, full, and challenging realities of little children, demanding jobs, petty squabbles, worry over despondent teens, bills to pay, and all sorts of other seemingly unspiritual aspects of family life.

COMMON CHALLENGES FAMILIES FACE

Technology and Family Life

Technology is here to stay. It will only increase and accelerate into our lives. The question is how to use it effectively. How can we take charge of it rather than have it take charge of us? We can ask ourselves how a new technology may assist and serve our family, then determine how and what we incorporate into our lives. Just as we manage the use of the car, the television, the foods within our home, and the space within our dwelling, we can also manage current and new technology, making adjustments as needed.

Recently a middle-aged couple told me about their struggle to raise their two teenagers. Their sixteen-year-old son had so many projects requiring computer use that his parents were never sure if he was legitimately working on schoolwork or playing games. In school, teachers face a similar dilemma with students using their hand-held devices. Even more importantly, these technologies are mostly solitary activities that, when used inappropriately or without moderation, take away from essential family interaction. Parent-child time, so necessary for family health and development, gets usurped by the TV or solitary computer time.

Again technology, like so many other things, is only one of a plethora of considerations parents face today without or with only limited experience from which to draw. We

"WE WILL AND DO MAKE MISTAKES."

will and do make mistakes. It is important to rectify them as they become apparent, always keeping in mind that what we are primarily seeking is a balance in our family life and one where we learn to help one another to grow in our capacities to love.

PARISH SUPPORTS FOR THE FAMILY

Just as God does, so too does the institutional Church have a huge stake in marital success. If the ecclesial Church is going to be fully successful in making disciples of our Lord, it needs to have people who know how to have a relationship with Jesus. Logically these same people will need to be people capable of having relationships in which one knows how to care, to listen, to compromise, to forgive, and to love. These relationship skills are the very things that are best learned within family life.

A couple once spoke to me of how little time and energy they typically had left for each other over the course of a given week. Couples often know when their marital relationship is suffering from neglect. Ideally the local parish could be a valuable resource in providing forums and parent classes, as well as offering guidance, insight, and mutual support. Marriage theology has reawakened an emphasis on marriage as a covenant relationship, rather than as a contractual one. Covenant, a much older word for sacrament, concerns promises made between spouses before God and community. Within this promise is an ongoing and open-ended pledge to "have and to hold" one's spouse throughout their shared lifetime as a couple. Interpersonal love is central to our current understanding of marriage, and the love called for is comprehensive. This marital love opens up the married couple to God's presence in the center of their union. The deep interrelationship between love of God and love of neighbor are played out in a loving marriage.

Parents need to see the need to slow down and take action. They must acknowledge what they can do for themselves as well. All of us need to wake up and then grow up. Waking up is about becoming

"PARENTS NEED TO SEE THE NEED TO SLOW DOWN AND TAKE ACTION."

conscious, which cannot happen when we are always on the go. Working two or three jobs, either as a couple or as a single parent, and raising a family, is taxing. Tired, joyless parents give children the unspoken message: "Grow up so that you, too, can eventually become a joyless and exhausted person like me." Our words have power, but our actions still speak louder. Responsible parents require respite care. It cannot wait "until after the children grow up." I have spoken to many parents with school-aged children who have never gone away for an overnight without their children. Toward the end of a recent annual marriage enrichment program, one of the wives present spoke out to those gathered. She expressed her frustration that, as good as the evening had been for her and her husband, she remained disappointed that the Church does so little to promote and support marriage in any consistent and ongoing way. This woman then made a bold and prophetic statement. She said, "I realize that if we're ever going to have our marriages supported and strengthened, it's really up to us to do it." She is absolutely correct. Family people need to take responsibility to see to it that marriage enrichment and family support happen in the parish either by demanding it and/or by initiating it.

- How can our parish better foster the mission of the Christian family?
- What would Vocation Sunday/Weekend be like if the parish fostered all vocations, including sacramental marriage?

MAKING TIME TO MAKE TIME

Twenty-first-century parents and married folks are found on the sidelines of sports fields, driving to and from classes, carrying side dishes to parish gatherings, in grocery stores late at night buying birthday treats for a child's class, volunteering for school trips, attending parent-teacher conferences, or shopping for some home-repair project. Married couples are often passing each other going to and coming from one or more jobs. On Sundays they're seen rushing late into Mass, their minds filled with distractions. They are not slackers. In fact, they work very hard attempting to raise their children well. But these frenetically paced lives focused only on making it through the day can lead to trouble and turmoil in the family.

The honest ones will tell you "something is amiss." They'll admit to their yearning for a slower-paced life, deeper friendships, downtime with children, and time to be a couple. If there is a tendency toward the selfish and materialistic life, most people come to recognize this as empty and unfulfilling. Implicit

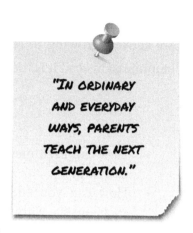

"IN ORDINARY AND EVERYDAY WAYS, PARENTS TEACH THE NEXT GENERATION."

in this lack of fulfillment are low expectations for marriage. The modern Catholic vision for marriage and family calls for relationships between husbands and wives to be a "communion." This is both a physical and emotional connection. Families are called to address injustices within and outside their family life. They do so by ordinary works of charity, mercy, and hospitality. Families claim their own identity as domestic churches whenever they pray and adapt family rituals, and whenever parents speak out against sexual exploitation or oppose violence to resolve conflict. In ordinary and everyday ways, parents teach the next generation, whether by assisting children to share their toys, helping a sick parishioner with a meal, snow removal, or lawn care, driving an elderly neighbor, volunteering at a local soup kitchen, or donating to local, national and international needs.

When husbands and wives take time to nurture their intimate relationships, when parents and children support each other and challenge each other to value all life, and when families open themselves to being in "communion" with the needy and are actively growing in faith together, there is hardly room for emptiness. Instead it is the road to fullness—to "life to the full."

- How can each member of your family work to serve each other?
- How can you encourage your family to engage in social justice within the parish?
- What are some ways your family can contribute in your neighborhood or the larger community?

Starting Now

PRAY WITH YOUR FAMILY

Prayer is foundationally important. It is a great starting point. Families need help to make prayer more embedded into their busy life and to take on this essential need for daily and weekly prayer. Prayer "on the go," in the car, at mealtimes, at bedtime, while exercising, even while shopping is possible and can become a practice like brushing one's teeth (yes, even pray while brushing your teeth!). Such are more typical ways for families to integrate prayer into their lives. Lengthier and other meaningful prayer experiences (like the rosary, *lectio divina*, Liturgy of the Hours) can also be integrated into family prayer time, but these kinds of experiences might have to build up with your family or may need some compromising (like only saying one decade of the rosary at night) based on time and children's attention spans. What's important isn't the number of hours spent in prayer, but that your family has a foundation of prayer to build on and rely on, a method of encountering God in life. This familial spirituality has been called the "spirituality of dirty diapers and dirty dishes."

"THIS FAMILIAL SPIRITUALITY HAS BEEN CALLED THE 'SPIRITUALITY OF DIRTY DIAPERS AND DIRTY DISHES.'"

Even parents need reminding that they are God's beloved. From this knowledge, they can pass on to their children this important instruction. Being God's beloved is what gives us purpose. The Christian family expresses godly love in the world—starting with one's spouse, children, and continuing out to neighbors, parishioners, the larger community, and the world. This is precisely what makes the universe a friendly place. If we can point these things out and acknowledge the presence of our Creator, we can go a long way.

- Do I know who I am as God's beloved?
- Do I express God's love in the world?
- How am I building a foundation of prayer for my family?
- How can silence and reflection time be seen as prayer and incorporated into our family life?
- Where are the places to incorporate more family prayer time?

EAT TOGETHER

Family meals provide an opportunity to utilize a contemporary version of St. Ignatius of Loyola's Examen: "What are you most grateful for (your consolation) and least grateful for (your desolation) today?" This excellent dinnertime prayer and conversation opens the door for a rich and meaningful dialogue with family members. You can engage children by simply asking them to share their "high" and "low" for that day. This sharing of each family member's moments of gratitude and lack of gratitude is more intimate than one may suspect. It also teaches family members to listen to each other and aids in the bond and connection. Married couples can also share the Examen prayer experience as a way to end each day.

"Rub-a-dub-dub, thanks for the grub! Yeah, God!" Mealtime, while perhaps less often for families with older children, provides opportunities to be together as a community. It is a natural time to pray and to communicate with each other. Meal blessings and shared prayer can enrich this time and open up to a family discussion. Letting each child open with his or her favorite prayer or light a candle are simple ways to engaged fuller participation. Also remembering to lower expectations and be grateful when the mealtime was positive will help when things don't always work out.

Given our family life stage, what are practical things we can do to better make use of our mealtimes?

- How can we promote engaged conversations as a family?
- What are some possible fun things we can include at mealtimes?
- What are topics we may wish to use for discussions at our meal times?

CELEBRATE THE HOLY DAY

Going to Mass as a family is preferable over everyone going at different times or not at all. A ritual of doughnuts, family breakfast, or even an occasional breakfast out can help persuade a reluctant teen to attend Sunday Mass. If teens say Mass or homilies are "boring" or they complain they don't feel welcomed at the parish, pay attention. Listen to their critique. If possible, try to do something about this. See if your parish offers a family, youth, or children's Mass in order for your children to better participate. A family-friendly Mass may have young children dismissed during the regular homily time for a children's homily and activity. See if there are opportunities for your teen to get involved by joining a youth group, choir, working as an usher or lector, or anything else that might pique his or her interest.

Families can serve together as hospitality ministers at the parish and take on extending a gracious welcome to all as they arrive. Coffee and doughnuts following weekend Masses is an opportunity to make all feel welcomed, including children.

Welcome and hospitality are the hallmarks of evangelization. This is the entire parish community's responsibility. Children need to feel welcome, just as the stranger does. Parents are their children's advocates at institutions such as schools, hospitals, and

- Can we discuss the homily or Scripture reading on the way home?
- Can we take on the ministry of hospitality as a family?
- What do our children wish to tell us regarding liturgical worship?
- What challenges do you face?

sports activities, so why not at the parish as well?

The Christian family life is not static. It is constantly in process as it moves through various stages. It's essential to pair each stage of needs with corresponding resources. New parents have different needs from parents of teens, or aging couples, and so on. It's important to reflect on your family life as you and the rest of your family grow. It's OK, even necessary, to change tactics and priorities as life requires.

Children do best when their parents are each able to take care

"THE CHRISTIAN FAMILY LIFE IS NOT STATIC."

of themselves and know how to love their children's mother or father. With divorced parents, the children do best when the parents manage to heal and forgive their former spouse, and move into coparenting without pulling their children into taking sides. Once you've determined the challenges your family faces, it's easier to see what you need to add, subtract, or modify to keep your family focused on God and each other. Take quiet time to listen to how God is calling you to grow in wisdom and grace.

The following are questions to ask yourself, your spouse, and your children to determine where you need to start.

Families

CONVERSATION STARTERS FOR FAMILIES:

1. What do we do regularly that makes you happy? What could we add to make you happy?
2. What is my favorite time(s) we have had together this year?
3. When did I first realize my family loves me? What caused this realization?
4. What makes me unique? What is a quality about our family that makes us unique?
5. How does our faith/religious practice assist us?
6. What is one thing I especially like about our family life?

CONVERSATION STARTERS FOR SPOUSES:

1. What do I do regularly that makes you happy? What other things could I also do to make you happy?
2. What is my favorite time(s) we had together this week/month/year?
3. What do I look forward to doing together as a couple?
4. When did I first realize I loved you and wanted to marry you?
5. What do I think about our sex life?
6. How does our faith/religious practice assist us?
7. What do we have in common? Which of our differences do I think complement each other?

DONALD J. PAGLIA and his wife, Chris, are codirectors of the Family Life Office of the Archdiocese of Hartford, CT.

FAMILY, THE BODY, AND GOD'S PLAN:

FOSTERING FAITH-FILLED SEXUALITY IN THE SECULAR WORLD

CHRISTOPHER WEST

LOVING AS GOD DOES

In a book devoted to exploring family issues, listing a chapter called on the family and sexuality among other chapters might lead one to believe that sexuality is just one topic among many related to the family. But that would be to miss the foundational significance of sexuality to the family. Every topic related to the family flows back, in one way or another, to the topic of sexuality because, without the sexual difference and without sexual union, there is no family.

Saint John Paul II, in his typical scholarly language, described the sexual union as the "ontological core" of the family. Ontology is the study of "being," the study of the deepest essence and reality of things. To speak of sexuality is to explore the very essence and core of what the family is, where and how it originates, and how it is ordered in its very being. To put it simply: "family" is the fruit, for good or for ill, of how we understand and live out our sexuality. Inasmuch as we embrace and live the splendor and beauty of God's plan for our sexuality, the family flourishes. Inasmuch as we fail to live God's plan for our sexuality, the family suffers, often greatly.

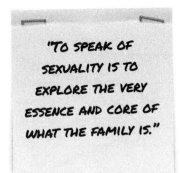

"TO SPEAK OF SEXUALITY IS TO EXPLORE THE VERY ESSENCE AND CORE OF WHAT THE FAMILY IS."

In this chapter, we will turn to St. John Paul II's marvelous *Theology of the Body (TOB)* in order to reclaim the splendor and beauty of God's plan for sexuality and, in this way, reclaim the deepest essence and foundation of the family.

WHAT MAKES THE BODY "THEOLOGICAL"?

To many Christians, the phrase "theology of the body" sounds like a contradiction in terms. We tend to have "the study of God" in one mental box and the human body in an entirely different one. But such a perspective only serves to demonstrate how the fundamental truths of our faith have yet to impact the way we engage the world.

If we take the truth of Christmas seriously, recognizing our bodies as a "study of God" will become as familiar as Grandma's figgy pudding. As John Paul II observed, "Through the fact

that the Word of God became flesh the body entered theology...
through the main door." We cannot see God; he is pure spirit.
But the astounding claim of Christianity is that the invisible God
has made himself visible through the human body. For in Christ
"dwells the whole fullness of the deity bodily" (Colossians 2:9).

God's mystery revealed in human flesh, "theology of the
body": This phrase isn't just the title of St. John Paul II's great
teaching. It represents the very logic of the Christian faith.

IMAGE OF GOD

In order to reveal the eternal mystery of his love, God speaks to
us in sign language. And the original sign that reveals his love
is the human body. The pope's thesis statement proclaims that
"only the body is capable of making visible what is invisible: the
spiritual and the divine. It has been created to transfer into the
visible reality of the world, the mystery hidden from eternity in
God, and thus to be a sign of it."

God wanted to transfer his mystery from heaven to earth.
That mystery is the eternal exchange of life-giving love and
communion found among Father, Son, and Holy Spirit. God
"transfers" this mystery to earth by making us in his image as
male and female. The purpose of the image, John Paul II tells us,
is to represent the original model. Think about it: a man's body
makes no sense by itself, nor does a woman's. Seen in light of each
other, we discover the unmistakable plan of the Creator. Man and
woman are designed to be a gift to each other, and, in the normal
course of events, the communion of the "two" leads to a "third."

Here, in a way, we see an image of the Trinity, a sign of the mystery hidden in God from eternity. In fact, to say that the body is "theological" is simply another way of saying that we're made in the image of God. Of course, none of this means that God is "sexual." We use spousal love only as an analogy to help us understand something of God's mystery. God's mystery, itself, remains infinitely beyond any human imagining.

IMAGE OF CHRIST'S LOVE FOR THE CHURCH

If imaging the love of the Trinity weren't astounding enough, sexuality is also a sign that reveals the "great mystery" of Christ's love for the Church. In fact, the Bible uses spousal love more than any other image to help us understand God's love for us. It begins in Genesis with the marriage of man and woman and ends in Revelation with the marriage of Christ and the Church. And right in the middle of the Bible we discover the glorious, erotic love poetry of the Song of Songs.

Here—in the beginning, end, and middle of the Bible—we find the interpretive key for understanding the whole of Scripture: God wants to marry us! But there's more! Remember what we learned in second grade: first comes love, then comes marriage, then comes the baby in the baby carriage. What we didn't realize was we were reciting some profound theology. God not only loves us; God not only wants to marry us; he wants us to "conceive" eternal life within us. And it's not mere poetry. In Mary, we see a woman who literally conceived divine life in her womb.

What we learn in the *TOB* is that God wanted this great "marital plan" to be so plain to us that he impressed an image of it right in our bodies by creating us male and female and calling us to become "one flesh." This is the story our bodies tell. It all comes together for us in Ephesians 5. Here, St. Paul quotes directly from Genesis: "'For this reason a man shall leave [his] father and [his] mother and be joined to his wife, and the two shall become one flesh.'" Then, linking the original marriage with the ultimate marriage, he adds: "This is a great mystery, but I speak in reference to Christ and the church" (Ephesians 5:31–32).

Christ is the new Adam who left his Father in heaven and the home of his mother on earth to give up his body for his bride (the Church) so that we might become one flesh with him. Where do we become one with the flesh of Christ? We do so most profoundly in the Eucharist. By receiving Christ's body into our own, we "conceive" eternal life in us. Saint Paul wasn't kidding when he described our sexuality as a "great mystery."

Image of the divine? Sounds great in theory, but it's a far cry from the way sex plays itself out in the experience of real human beings. Skyrocketing rates of adultery and divorce; unwed mothers and fatherless children; the casual hookup culture; the tragedy of rape and other heinous sex crimes, even against children; AIDS and a host of other sexually transmitted diseases; sex trafficking and a multibillion dollar pornography industry; not to mention the general cloud of shame and guilt that often hangs over sexual matters. All of this paints a very different picture. The picture it paints is the tragedy of human sinfulness.

IN THE BEGINNING

Facebook lists more than fifty "genders" to choose from when making one's personal profile. Christ's words cut through this chaos and confusion like a knife: "Have you not read that from the beginning the Creator 'made them

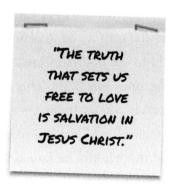

"THE TRUTH THAT SETS US FREE TO LOVE IS SALVATION IN JESUS CHRIST."

male and female'" (Matthew 19:4)? If men and women are blind to the truth of their sexuality and plagued in their relationships with all kinds of difficulties, Christ wants to remind us that "from the beginning it was not so" (Matthew 19:8). And here's the good news St. John Paul II proclaims from the rooftops in his *TOB*: Christ came into the world to make God's original plan a reality in our lives.

With this approach—the Gospel approach—the pope shifts the discussion about sexual morality from legalism ("How far can I go before I break the law?") to liberty ("What is the truth about sex that sets me free to love?"). The truth that sets us free to love is salvation in Jesus Christ.

But what kind of "love" are we talking about? Here the Greek terms *eros* and *agape* are very helpful. Eros refers to human, sexual love, while agape refers to divine, sacrificial love. In the beginning, there was no conflict between these loves. Indeed, God placed eros in the human heart as the power to express agape. In other words, God created erotic desire as the power to love as he loves. And this is how the first couple experienced it.

We know this because the first man and woman were "naked, yet they felt no shame" (Genesis 2:25). They understood and lived their sexuality in the image of God, and there is no shame in that. Nakedness without shame, in fact, is the key to understanding God's original plan for human life. It unlocks the intimacy and ecstasy of love that God intended in the beginning.

The entrance of shame, then, indicates the dawn of lust, of eros cut off from agape. Lust, John Paul tells us, seeks the "sensation of sexuality" apart from the truth of love. We cover our bodies in a fallen world not because they're bad, but to protect their inherent goodness from the degradation of lust. Because we know we're made for divine love, we feel instinctively threatened not only by overt lustful behavior but also even by a lustful look.

THE REDEMPTION OF SEXUALITY

Christ's words are severe in this regard. He insists that if we look lustfully at others, we've already committed adultery in our hearts (see Matthew 5:28). John Paul asks whether we should fear these words, or have confidence in their power to save us. Christ's words about lust are not a condemnation of erotic desire. Instead they are a call, John Paul tells us, to experience the "fullness of eros," which he describes as "the upward impulse of the human spirit toward what is true, good, and beautiful."

We needn't merely cope with our lusts or manage our sinful tendencies. Our sexual desires can be effectively transformed through the "redemption of our bodies" (Romans 8:23). Living a redeemed sexuality is very different from repressing sexuality. As we allow our lusts to be crucified with Christ (see Galatians 5:24), we also come to experience the resurrection of sexual desire according to God's original plan.

C.S. Lewis shares a powerful image of this death and resurrection of desire at the end of his book *The Great Divorce*. Before a certain "human ghost" can enter heaven, he must contend with his lust, symbolized by a lizard perched on his shoulder. When the Angel of Fire who guards the eternal gates asks to slay the lizard, we can all relate to the ghost's long list of excuses: not today; the gradual process is better; it will hurt too much; let me get an opinion from another doctor, and so forth. After honestly reckoning with what lust has done in his life, the ghost finally grants permission and the angel breaks the lizard's neck, flinging it to the ground.

Immediately the ghost takes on radiant flesh, a resurrected man, and pure love flows out of him "like liquid," says Lewis. But that's not even the best part. The lizard is also resurrected—now transformed into a great white stallion with a tail and mane of gold. The gates of heaven open, the resurrected man mounts the stallion, and redeemed eros itself is what enables him to climb the "impossible steeps" of life everlasting.

We might say that God gave us eros in the beginning to be like the power of a rocket to launch us toward the stars. Sin has inverted our rocket engines causing us to crash and burn. The gospel does not condemn eros. Rather, it redirects our rocket engines toward heaven.

THE ETERNAL MARRIAGE

Of course, on this side of heaven, we'll always be able to recognize a battle in our hearts between love and lust. Only in eternity will the battle cease, as will marriage as we know it. Recall that Christ said we will no longer marry in the resurrection (see Matthew 22:30). But this doesn't mean our longing for union will be obliterated. It means it will be fulfilled in the "wedding day of the Lamb" (Revelation 19:7).

"It is emblematic," says Pope Francis, "how in the Book of Revelation, John, taking up the intuition of the Prophets, describes the final, definitive dimension [of our existence]…as a bride adorned for her husband' (Revelation 21:2). Here is what awaits us!" exclaims Francis. "And here, then, is who the Church is…a bride with her bridegroom. And it is not just a manner of speaking: they will be real and true nuptials! Yes, because Christ …has truly wed us and has made us, as a people, his bride. This is nothing more than the fulfillment of the plan of communion and love woven by God throughout history…."

If the one flesh union is a sign of our eternal destiny, we'll no longer need a sign to point us to heaven when we're in heaven. But nothing of what is true, good, and beautiful about the union of the sexes, marriage, and family life will be obliterated in heaven. Rather, it will be taken up, transformed, glorified, and fulfilled beyond our wildest imaginings in the marriage of Christ and the Church and in the family of God (the communion of the saints).

SEXUALITY AND THE CHRISTIAN VOCATIONS

Only by understanding the ultimate truth about sexuality do we gain a proper understanding of the Christian vocations of celibacy and marriage. Both vocations are a call to live the most profound truth of who we are as sexual beings.

When lived authentically, Christian celibacy isn't a rejection of sexuality. It's a living out of the ultimate purpose and meaning of sexuality: to point us to union with God. Those who sacrifice marriage "for the sake of the kingdom" (Matthew 19:12) do so in order to devote all of their energies and desires to the marriage that alone can satisfy, the marriage of Christ and the Church. In a way, they're "skipping" the sacrament (the earthly sign) in anticipation of the ultimate reality.

> "ONLY BY UNDERSTANDING THE ULTIMATE TRUTH ABOUT SEXUALITY DO WE GAIN A PROPER UNDERSTANDING OF THE CHRISTIAN VOCATIONS OF CELIBACY AND MARRIAGE."

In a different way, marriage also anticipates heaven. "In the joys of their love and family life," the *Catechism* tells us that God gives spouses "here on earth a foretaste of the wedding feast of the Lamb" (*CCC* 1642). However, in order for marriage to bring the happiness it is meant to bring, spouses must contend diligently with the effects of sin.

Marriage does not justify lust. Rather, eros is meant to express agape: "Husbands, love your wives, even as Christ loved the church" (Ephesians 5:25). Christ loved the Church freely, totally, faithfully, and fruitfully. This is exactly what spouses commit to at the altar. "Have you come here freely?" the priest asks, "to give yourselves to each other without reservation? Do you promise to be faithful all the days of your lives? Do you promise to receive children lovingly from God?" Bride and groom say "yes."

In turn, spouses are meant to express this same "yes" with their bodies whenever they become one flesh. Sexual intercourse is meant to be a renewal of wedding vows, where the words of the marriage commitment are made flesh.

LIVING AS TRUE PROPHETS

The Church's sexual ethic begins to make complete sense when viewed through this lens. It's not a prudish list of prohibitions. It's a call to live the love we're created for. It's a call to embrace our own greatness and destiny. It's a call to live as true prophets.

A true prophet is one who proclaims God's love truthfully. This is what the body and sexual union are meant to do. However, if we can speak the truth with our bodies, we can also speak lies. Ultimately all questions of sexual morality come down to one simple question: Does this truly image God's free, total, faithful, fruitful love or does it not? In practical terms, how healthy would a marriage be if spouses were regularly unfaithful to their vows? On the

"ASK YOURSELF: DOES THIS TRULY IMAGE GOD'S FREE, TOTAL, FAITHFUL, FRUITFUL LOVE, OR DOES IT NOT?"

other hand, how healthy would a marriage be if spouses regularly renewed their vows, expressing an ever-increasing commitment to them? This is what is at stake in the Church's teaching on sexual morality.

Masturbation, fornication, adultery, intentionally sterilized sex, homosexual acts—none of these image God's free, total, faithful, and fruitful love. None of these behaviors express and renew wedding vows. They aren't marital and, knowingly or unknowingly, they turn those who engage in them into false prophets.

Is this said to condemn anyone? Absolutely not. It's said to save us all. Very, very few of us have ever heard the "why" behind the "what" of Catholic teaching presented in a compelling way. We must be very patient with those who haven't been taught or understood Catholic teaching in this regard, beginning with ourselves. At the same time, we must commit ourselves to growing in our understanding of the theology of our bodies and to living it out more fully. Parents have a special responsibility in this regard. Children learn far more from their parents' example than from their words. When parents embrace the demands of living as true prophets and witness joyfully to the splendor of God's plan for sexual love, their children are much more likely to embrace those demands as well.

LIVING THE THEOLOGY OF OUR BODIES

Those who seek to live out the theology of their bodies are sure to encounter a great spiritual battle. Ponder this for a moment:

if the union of the sexes is the main sign in this world of our call to union with God, and if there is an enemy who wants to keep us from union with God, where do you think he's going to aim his most poisonous arrows? Saint John Paul II observed that "the family is placed at the center of the great struggle between good and evil, between life and death, between love and all that is opposed to love."

How do we win this battle? We must put on the armor of God, says St. Paul. And the first piece of armor is with our "loins girded in truth" (Ephesians 6:14). Living our sexuality "truthfully" is so critical that, according to St. John Paul, it determines "a good or bad lot" not just in the dimension of family life, but "in the dimension of life as a whole."

How do we gird our loins with the truth? John Paul II says we are called "first of all" to make this "theology of the body" the content of our lives and behavior. How do we do that? Here are some practical suggestions of ways to keep the *TOB* at the core of your life and as the core of your family.

Take up an ongoing study of St. John Paul II's *TOB*. There are a great many books, DVDs, seminars, and courses available by many insightful teachers. (If you like my approach, you can receive ongoing formation at corproject.com. I also teach week-long courses through the Theology of the Body Institute at tobinstitute.org).

Develop and deepen a daily prayer life. According to John Paul, prayer is one of three "infallible and indispensable" means for living the *TOB*. Prayer, Pope Benedict XVI tells us, means learning how to direct all the deepest desires of our heart for love ("eros") to the Lord, seeking "nuptial union" with him. Prayer, therefore, is an exercise of *desire*. *Time for God* and *Thirsting for Prayer*, both by Jacque Philippe, are two books I've found very helpful for developing my prayer life.

Frequent the sacrament of confession. This is another "infallible and indispensable" means for living the *TOB*, says John Paul. Confession is not only where we expose our sins and receive forgiveness. It's also where we expose our hurts, faults, fears, and wounds, getting utterly "naked" before God in order to receive his healing love. If we want to be the men and women God created us to be, we should be going to confession at least once a month.

Frequent the sacrament of the Eucharist. This is the final "infallible and indispensable" means for living the *TOB*. If prayer is where we open our desire, and confession is where we get "naked," the Eucharist is where we consummate the union. The Eucharist is the very source of the love that we are called to share in marriage and family life. We can't give what we haven't received.

Speak openly and honestly with your children. Everyone experiences a hunger to know the meaning of sexuality. If that hunger is not fed from the beauty and richness of God's banquet, your children will seek to satisfy that hunger elsewhere. You can be confident that if you are taking up an ongoing study of the *Theology of the Body,* deepening your prayer life, and frequenting the sacraments of confession and Eucharist, you will be well-equipped to educate your children in the glories of God's plan for sexuality.

There will be no renewal of the family without a return to God's plan for our sexuality. But that will never happen unless we rediscover that the Church's teaching on sexuality is not the prudish list of prohibitions it's assumed to be. Rather, it is an invitation to the banquet of love for which every human being yearns.

That is what St. John Paul's *TOB* offers us. If we commit ourselves to learning it, living it, and sharing it with others, we will not fall short of renewing the face of the earth.

CHRISTOPHER WEST is a husband and father of five. His global lecturing, multiple books, courses, study programs, and media appearances have also made him the world's most recognized teacher of St. John Paul II's *Theology of the Body*. Learn more at corproject.com.

DON'T PANIC:

WHEN WILL
MY FAMILY
BE PERFECT?

GREG + JENNIFER
WILLITS

HELPFUL STEPS

Because of the thousands of hours of radio, podcast, television, and online video projects our family has created since 2005, it sometimes feels like we've positioned ourselves under a microscope for all to see. One of our biggest concerns when doing these shows is that we'll somehow come off as overly pious or that we're trying to come off as the perfect family when, in reality, that would be far from the truth.

Our initial forays into media were nothing more than technological experiments. Nothing could have adequately prepared us for the response we received to the candid sharing of our experiences with unemployment, miscarriages, and

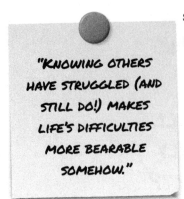

"KNOWING OTHERS HAVE STRUGGLED (AND STILL DO!) MAKES LIFE'S DIFFICULTIES MORE BEARABLE SOMEHOW."

struggling with our faith. With this sharing came one of the greatest lessons we've ever learned: there are many people in this world who feel completely inadequate as individuals, as family units, and even as Christians. Finding others in similar situations—companions on the journey to heaven—is somehow comforting, reassuring, and motivational.

Knowing others have struggled (and still do!) makes life's difficulties more bearable somehow. That's why there are so many support groups in the world today. We all need help with something.

When we wrote our first book, *The Catholics Next Door*, we immediately knew the subtitle had to be *Adventures in Imperfect Living*. Why? Because we're all imperfect even though we're called to seek perfection, as Jesus prays in John 17:23. So if you feel like you're a bad husband or a bad wife, if you're certain that your family is completely messed up, if you feel like you're the most miserable sinner around, take comfort in knowing that you're not alone. We often feel that way, too.

Our family, as well as yours, was first modeled in the image and likeness of the Holy Trinity. One could argue that our families are formed from the very blueprints of God's perfection. We are called by our "perfect" creation to make our families places that reflect this profound relationship of life and love that exists

THE REAL WORLD Don't Panic ✖ 147

between the three persons of the Trinity—Father, Son, and Holy Spirit. In working toward this perfection, our family becomes a domestic church where the will of God takes precedence and where he is worshiped and adored at the center of our lives.

You might be wondering how in the world can you lead your family to this spiritually rich and God-centered household? How do you combine all these elements of a "Catholic family" into the reality of your family? We wondered, too. So with lots of prayer and careful consideration, coupled with the truth that each family has its own unique characteristics, personalities, income, and cultural norms, we have prepared five easy-to-implement suggestions based on our experience to help you put it all together. Hopefully this gives you and your family a starting point on your own journey toward holiness, whatever that looks like.

FIRST: EAT, DRINK, AND BE MERRY TOGETHER

Is it any accident that God instituted the Eucharist to bring his flock together? We are so used to partaking of the Body and Blood of our Lord in the form of bread and wine at Mass that we sometimes forget the everyday action of eating and drinking together is also a God-sanctioned activity that brings about another kind of holy communion. Sharing meals together in the home has the same bonding effect on families.

A family meal is one of the best ways to draw everyone to the same location for a common purpose. How you spend that time sharing with each other is up to you, but the potential for powerful bonding is as easy as, well, pie.

Don't underestimate the seeds that can be planted in the hearts and minds of your family around good food. Put some thought into interesting conversations you know will garner the attention of your family. The "How was work/school?" question is great to start, but not always revealing. We are taught that the more we take the time to know Jesus, the more we will love him. This works the same way for your family. Take the time to get to know individual interests and start mealtime conversations that will keep everyone engaged. When your family takes this time to connect, you'll be building love and respect. And that's a great foundation as you begin your family's journey to holiness.

But what if your dinner scene is chaos at best? From screaming toddlers to back-talking teens, it can be a challenge to eat in each other's presence, let alone use that time to build relationships. In our house, it takes at least ten minutes just to get everyone gathered around for the family meal. And in those ten minutes there's chaos, and scrambling, and bickering, and usually one or two of us start getting impatient with the lack of organization and our growing hunger. As soon as we notice at least a majority of our family within range of the table (and before anyone can realize that someone forgot to grab the salt shaker), our oldest son—desperate to start eating—takes it upon himself to loudly proclaim (with just a hint of annoyance), "BLESS US, OH LORD, FOR THESE THY GIFTS WHICH WE ARE ABOUT TO RECEIVE...."

Often, funny conversation erupts but other times not. Sometimes the teens eat and run, other times they stay and share interesting bits from their day.

Sometimes we talk about matters of faith, other times we'll talk about pop-culture news. Sometimes we won't speak at all. Sometimes the inevitable arguments erupt between siblings. But regardless of what does or does not happen, there is always togetherness and communion. During this one meal we can all come together with our imperfections to partake of the family feast. In this small way, we are mirroring the eucharistic experience right in our dining room with our closest brothers and sisters in Christ: our family.

"WE CAN ALL COME TOGETHER WITH OUR IMPERFECTIONS TO PARTAKE OF THE FAMILY FEAST."

SECOND: SAFEGUARD WHAT ENTERS YOUR HOME

Like a good meal satisfies our body, a well told story satisfies our heart and mind. In St. John Paul II's March 17, 1995, address to the Plenary Assembly of the Pontifical Commission for Social Communications, he states, "The film industry has become a universal medium exercising a profound influence on the development of people's attitudes and choices, and possessing a remarkable ability to influence public opinion and culture across all social and political frontiers." This is glorious news as much as it is a stern warning.

We are living in a time in which the screens that deliver our entertainment and allow us access to the Internet have become staples in most U.S. households. More screens in the home means more opportunities for positive and negative influences on the hearts and minds of our kids (and ourselves). The reality is we can't just count the number of televisions or computers anymore. Any device can bring the media and influencers into your home. It just needs access to your household's internet service. Because we have personal and professional experience creating media, we love and encourage interacting with it, but that interaction comes with great caution.

We can't ignore the fact that interacting with media influences us. When your children are young, parental controls make this easier to regulate. Your children can only watch programs or play the video games you allow. For the first eight to ten years of your kids' life, the task of moderating is fairly easy. From there, children begin to flex their need-for-independence muscles and start testing parental decisions. But if you stay in their business regularly and correct them when they stray, by the time your children become older teens and young adults, they will have the skills required to make informed decisions on what is and isn't appropriate material to let into their life.

Safeguarding the internet that comes into your home is something we strongly recommend you take the time to learn about. With our existing software and hardware setup, combined with the use of free services like OpenDNS (OpenDNS.com), we're able to keep pornography and other unwanted content off our network. When it comes to online gaming, we

> "THE BEST MEDICINE FOR HELPING TO STRENGTHEN YOUR FAMILY'S MORAL COMPASS IS REGULAR CONVERSATION."

moderate the computer time restrictions for the younger kids and give more freedom to the older ones as long as their grades are good, they are helpful to the needs of the family, and they show clear signs of growing spiritual development.

Most modern televisions and satellite/cable companies offer unique parental controls to help parents create appropriate restrictions based on the ages of young family members. This is awesome for parents of teens who like to stay up late and watch television without their parents knowing. Once they see the onscreen restriction warning (or better yet a required password for any shows over a certain rating), they know to move along because they can't ask us to key in the access code after we've gone to bed.

Being a tech-savvy parent has great advantages because you can't always be there to say no. If you have the equipment in your house programmed to honor your family's values, your kids are reminded of them even when you're not there.

Aside from setting up parental controls and restrictions, the best medicine for helping to strengthen your family's moral compass is regular conversation. Point out to your kids the problems with bad entertainment and websites. Openly and regularly discuss problematic content and lovingly explain what is and is not allowed in the house. Explain why this content is objectionable and use those moments to weave in reminders of Catholic teachings, especially on the dignity of the human person. Although it's tempting to keep our families shielded from the world and deny them access to anything questionable, we'll do them and the world a greater service by encouraging them to discern right from wrong on their own. Also, help them go to confession for those times when they've crossed the line and share with them our need for forgiveness and mercy.

THIRD: SERVE AT HOME AND BEYOND

As of the publication of this book, we have four sons and one daughter. One might assume that our family is able to supply a regular stream of altar servers for Mass, given that all of our sons are perfect serving age. What better way to publicly show your willingness to serve the Church than through this practice of altar serving?

The truth is, so far this activity has been a poor match for us and our children. We are very aware of what this looks like to the parish community, but there is nothing we can do to change what others may assume. Our reasons are known to God and our family. Does this make us bad parents? No. It just means we find other ways our kids can experience the benefits of serving others.

A great place to instill the value of serving others is in your own household. Start by showing children the value of chores and responsibilities within the home. Regular chores help children not only become more responsible but also lets them know they are a vital component in making the house run efficiently. Working together makes the family a cohesive unit.

A wonderful example of service from Scripture can be found in Luke 1:39–53. This section of Luke's Gospel recounts one amazing example of Mary's service. Mary leaves the privacy and safety of her home and travels a great distance to serve her older cousin Elizabeth, who was due to give birth in a few months. The primary spark that motivates Mary to serve so boldly is the conception of Jesus Christ in her womb. One moment Christ is placed in her womb; the next moment Mary is out helping someone in need.

"A GREAT PLACE TO INSTILL THE VALUE OF SERVING OTHERS IS RIGHT IN YOUR OWN HOUSEHOLD."

Remind your children that when you go to Mass they, too, are receiving Christ through his word and through his Body and Blood in the Eucharist. How can they choose to serve in their own, little or big, way inside or outside the home?

Finally, Jesus tells us in the Beatitudes (Matthew 5:7) that being merciful to someone will lead to supreme happiness. Serving the needs of others is a way for mercy to be extended toward them. In this light, you can see how serving leads to happiness. If you can prayerfully discern which types of service match your family's charism, you will be that much closer to developing a fruitful spirituality for every member of your family.

FOURTH: MODEL HEALTHY RELATIONSHIPS TO YOUR CHILDREN

Who doesn't want holy kids who are equipped to be in healthy relationships of their own? It's easy for us to lose sleep at night worrying over the fate of our children. The good news is that the relationships we model in front of our children have a dramatic impact on how they perceive they should behave in relationships of their own. If you show genuine contentment in your marriage, regardless of hardships, they will see an example of true love and be better able to replicate it on their own. Your example will become their reference point in the future. What your children see makes a tremendous difference in shaping their own ability to love as we are called to do by God and to feel loved in return.

In our family, we constantly make sure our kids see us spending time nurturing our Catholic faith and our personal relationships with Jesus Christ. In addition to going to Mass weekly with our family, we do our best to make God a part of our family discussions throughout the week. Our home is filled with visual reminders of our faith such as statues of the Holy Family and our Lady in common areas. In each child's bedroom is a crucifix and an image of the Sacred Heart of Jesus. We've provided Bibles for different age groups and in different styles to appeal to each child's individual personality. We push ourselves to do the best we can with the resources we have in visibly representing our Catholic faith in our household.

If you work hard at putting God at the forefront of what you do as a parent and as a family, God will guide you in this complex role. Realizing how God loves us through our faults is a powerful model for us to love our children through theirs.

Love can be modeled in many

> "REALIZING HOW GOD LOVES US THROUGH OUR FAULTS IS A POWERFUL MODEL FOR US TO LOVE OUR CHILDREN THROUGH THEIRS."

ways, through images of God's love for us, through loving and patient relationships with our children, and even through physical expressions of love between spouses. Let your kids see you holding hands, hugging, and sneaking a few kisses! Make sure you plan regular date nights for you and your spouse to stay connected to the love that existed before the children came. When possible, smile at each other. It's a small and simple act that shows kids all is well with mom and dad. Show your kids how to handle disagreements with each other by refraining from yelling and instead listening and responding to the other in kind.

If for some reason you are struggling with authentically loving your spouse, make this a priority. Seek the healing sacraments of our Church and if appropriate in your situation a mentor couple or counselor. Continue to engage in difficult conversations with your spouse and be prepared to listen. Do not attempt to sweep spousal resentments under the rug where hurts and wounds can fester in the dark. Allow the light of Christ to expose any hurts and, after much prayer, heal them.

Your entire family started with the love that existed between you as husband and wife, and with God. With God's help, your marriage will be strong.

FIFTH: PRAY AS A FAMILY

Family prayer sessions can be a huge challenge with little kids. We went through several years of hardship in this area. We desperately wanted to feel peaceful enlightenment with God during these moments but felt extreme exhaustion and frazzled nerves instead.

Having your entire family harmoniously joined together with heads neatly bowed as all members pray with united hearts and minds is a wonderful and worthy goal. (If you achieve that, please tell us how you managed it.)

Although we believe it's important to have a proper exterior posture while praying, it's more important to focus on the interior one. To help your children develop this skill, take the time to explain that meditation is a deliberate choice to think about Jesus more than yourself. Tell them how well you understand the challenge of putting God first in your thoughts. Explain that God's love for us is so intense he wants to give us the grace to meditate better and to be closer to him. We just have to ask.

We shouldn't approach family prayer with the attitude that we are somehow better or more enlightened than all other families. We should stay focused on the truth that as a family unit we are struggling to stay in a committed relationship with God every day. We have to be diligent to maintain that relationship. So, pray together as often as you can. Even if some members of the family are not able to join you for whatever reason, pray with whoever is available. Cling to God, our "Daddy," with every bit of your strength. The rewards you gain will far outweigh the effort you put in!

Will taking your family (sometimes kicking and screaming) on this tough road be easy to accomplish? No. But is it possible? YES! But don't take our word for it. Take God's.

> "WE SHOULD STAY FOCUSED ON THE TRUTH THAT AS A FAMILY UNIT WE ARE STRUGGLING TO STAY IN A COMMITTED RELATIONSHIP WITH GOD EVERY DAY."

Here are some powerful reminders of God's strength and encouragement whenever we want to achieve something seemingly impossible, like creating a perfect Catholic family:

Jesus looked at them and said, "For human beings this is impossible, but for God all things are possible" (Matthew 19:26).

"...for nothing will be impossible for God" (Luke 1:37).

I have the strength for everything through him who empowers me (Philippians 4:13).

"Amen, I say to you, if you have faith the size of a mustard seed, you will say to this mountain, 'Move from here to there,' and it will move. Nothing will be impossible for you" (Matthew 17:20).

"Therefore I tell you, all that you ask for in prayer, believe that you will receive it and it shall be yours" (Mark 11:24).

Do not fear: I am with you; do not be anxious: I am your God. I will strengthen you, I will help you, I will uphold you with my victorious right hand (Isaiah 41:10).

Ah, my Lord GOD! You made the heavens and the earth with your great power and your outstretched arm; nothing is too difficult for you (Jeremiah 32:17).

So there you have it. Eating together, safeguarding what comes into your home, serving, modeling healthy relationships, and praying with your family are great building blocks toward achieving your own holy family in this modern era. Stumbling on your way toward this holy goal is unavoidable but rewarding every time you get back on your feet. Remember, you are not alone in this journey.

Let's continue to pray not only for the betterment of our own families but also for the families around the world who are collectively struggling in their own ways.

"REMEMBER, YOU ARE NOT ALONE IN THIS JOURNEY."

GREG AND JENNIFER WILLITS have been married since 1995 and are the parents of four boys and a girl. They've co-founded multiple Catholic apostolates and currently host the popular weekly podcast *The Catholics Next Door,* which can be listened to free on GregandJennifer.com.

RESOURCES
AND WORKS
CONSULTED

FAMILY, SCRIPTURE, AND THE SACRAMENTS

- Apostolic Exhortation *Familiaris Consortio* of Pope John Paul II to the Episcopate, to the Clergy and to the Faithful of the Whole Catholic Church on the Role of the Christian Family in the Modern World. November 22, 1981.
- *Compendium of the Catechism of the Catholic Church.* Washington, D.C.: United States Conference of Catholic Bishops, 2006.
- Meeting with the Volunteers of the XXVIII World Youth Day, Address of Pope Francis. Twenty-eighth World Youth Day. Rio de Janeiro, Brazil. July 28, 2013.

CHURCH, FAMILY, AND WORKING TOGETHER

- Apostolic Exhortation *Familiaris Consortio* of Pope John Paul II to the Episcopate, to the Clergy and to the Faithful of the Whole Catholic Church on the Role of the Christian Family in the Modern World. November 22, 1981.
- Apostolic Exhortation *Evangelii Nuntiandi* of Pope Paul VI to the Episcopate, to the Clergy and to all the Faithful of the Entire World. December 8, 1975.
- *A Family Perspective in Church and Society.* 10th Anniversary ed. Washington, D.C.: U.S. Catholic Conference, 1998.

- *Follow the Way of Love: A Pastoral Message of the U.S. Catholic Bishops to Families.* Washington, D.C.: United States Catholic Conference, 1994.
- National Association of Catholic Family Life Ministers (NACFLM). Accessed July 13, 2015. Nacflm.org.
- Apostolic Exhortation *Evangelii Gaudium* of Pope Francis to the Bishops, Clergy, Consecrated Persons and the Lay Faithful on the Proclamation of the Gospel in Today's World. November 23, 2013.
- Pastoral Constitution on the Church in the Modern World, *Gaudium et Spes,* promulgated by Pope Paul VI. December 7, 1965.
- Smith, Christian, and Melinda Lundquist Denton. *Soul Searching: The Religious and Spiritual Lives of American Teenagers.* Oxford: Oxford University Press, 2005.
- Smith, Christian, and Patricia Snell. *Souls in Transition: The Religious and Spiritual Lives of Emerging Adults.* Oxford: Oxford University Press, 2009.
- Smith, Christian, and Kyle Longest, Jonathan Hill, Kari Christoffersen. *Young Catholic America: Emerging Adults In, Out of, and Gone from the Church.* Oxford: Oxford University Press, 2014.
- "Strong Catholic Family Faith." Accessed July 13, 2015. Catholicfamilyfaith.org.

CHANGING TIMES, CHANGING ROLES, SAME FAMILY

- [7]American Psychological Association. "Marriage and Divorce." Accessed July 14, 2015. Apa.org/topics/divorce/.
- [15]Allen, John. "Francis and the Culture of Encounter." *National Catholic Reporter,* December 20, 2013.
- [8]Banks, Adelle M. "Christians Question Divorce Rates of faithful." *USA Today,* March 14, 2011. Accessed July 14, 2015. Usatoday30.usatoday.com/news/religion/2011-03-14-divorce-christians_N.htm.
- *Catechism of the Catholic Church.* Washington, D.C.: United States Conference of Catholic Bishops, 1997, 2000.
- [2]Child Trends Data Bank. "Births to Unmarried Women." Last modified March 2015. Childtrends.org/?indicators=births-to-unmarried-women.
- [4]The Heritage Foundation. "Nearly 12 Percent of Couples Living Together Are Unmarried." Accessed July 14, 2015. Familyfacts.org/charts/110/nearly-12-percent-of-couples-living-together-are-unmarried.

- [11]Fowler, James. *Stages of Faith: The Psychology of Human Development and the Quest for Meaning.* San Francisco: HarperOne, 1995.
- [5,8]Gray, Mark M. "Sunday Morning: Deconstructing Catholic Mass Attendance in the 1950s and Now." *Nineteen Sixty-four Research Blog* (CARA). March 21, 2011. Nineteensixty-four.blogspot.com/2011/03/sunday-morning-deconstructing-catholic.html.
- [3]Greenwood, Jeremy, and Nezih Guner. "Marriage and Divorce Since WWII: Analyzing the Role of Technological Progress on the Formation of Households. In NBER Macroeconomics Annual 2008, edited by Daron Acemoglu, Kenneth Rogoff, and Michael Woodford, vol. 23, 231-236. Chicago: University of Chicago Press, 2009.
- Encyclical *Evangelium Vitae* to the Bishops, Priests and Deacons, Men and Women religious, lay Faithful, and all People of Good Will on the Value and Inviolability of Human Life. March 25, 1995.
- [3,9,10]Krogstad, Jens Manuel. "5 Facts about the Modern American Family." *Fact Tank News in the Numbers,* April 30, 2014. Accessed July 14, 2015. Pewresearch.org/fact-tank/2014/04/30/5-facts-about-the-modern-american-family/.
- [14]Marquardt, Elizabeth. *Between Two Worlds: The Inner Lives of Children of Divorce.* New York: Harmony, 2006.
- [14]Marquardt, Elizabeth. "Between Two Worlds: The Spiritual Lives of Children of Divorce." (Video presentation). January 15, 2013. Accessed July 14, 2015. Youtube.com/watch?v=wV0RJDU8LJ4.
- [6]Copen, Casey, and Kimberly Daniels, William D. Mosher. "First Pre-Marital Cohabitation in the United States: 2006-2010 National Survey of Family Growth." *National Health Statistics Report.* April 4, 2013.
- [1]Pappas, Stephanie. "5 Ways Motherhood has Changed Over Time." *Live Science,* May 10, 2013. Accessed July 14, 2015. Livescience. com/29521-5-ways-motherhood-has-changed.html.
- [13]Pargament, Kenneth I. (2011). *Spiritually Integrated Psychotherapy: Understanding and Addressing the Sacred.* New York: Guilford Press, 2011.
- [12]Pew Research Center. "'Nones' on the Rise." October 9, 2012. Accessed July 14, 2015. Pewforum.org/2012/10/09/nones-on-the-rise/.
- Popcak, Gregory K, and Lisa A. Popcak. *Discovering God Together: The Catholic Guide to Raising Faithful Kids.* Manchester, NH: Sophia Institute Press, 2015.
- [10]United States Department of Labor. "Latest Annual Data. Women of Working Age." Accessed July 14, 2015. Dol.gov/wb/stats/latest_annual_data.htm.

FAITH, FAMILY, AND FINDING THE TIME

- Apostolic Exhortation *Familiaris Consortio* of Pope John Paul II to the Episcopate, to the Clergy and to the Faithful of the Whole Catholic Church on the Role of the Christian Family in the Modern World. November 22, 1981.
- *Catechism of the Catholic Church.* Washington, D.C.: United States Conference of Catholic Bishops, 1997, 2000.
- United States Conference of Catholic Bishops. "For Your Marriage." Accessed July 14, 2015. Foryourmarriage.org.
- Hendey, Lisa M. "Catholic Mom." Accessed July 14, 2015. Catholicmom.com.
- Trinity Communications. "Catholic Culture." Accessed July 14, 2015. CatholicCulture.org.

FAITH, VOCATIONS, AND DISCERNMENT

- Bengtson, Vern. *CARA Report.* 2005.
- *Catechism of the Catholic Church.* Washington, D.C.: United States Conference of Catholic Bishops, 1997, 2000.
- Climacus, John. *The Ladder of Divine Ascent.* New York: Paulist Press, 1982.
- Dogmatic Constitution on the Church, *Lumen Gentium.* Promulgated by Pope Paul VI. November 21, 1964.
- Apostolic Exhortation *Evangelii Nuntiandi* of Pope Paul VI to the Episcopate, to the Clergy and to all the Faithful of the Entire World. December 8, 1975.
- John Paul II. *The Meaning of Vocation.* New York: Scepter Pubs, 1998.
- Wisdom, Andrew Carl, and Christine Kiley. *Tuning in to God's Call.* Liguori, MO: Liguori, 2012.

CHURCH, THE HOME, AND PUTTING IT TOGETHER

- Apostolic Exhortation *Familiaris Consortio* of Pope John Paul II to the Episcopate, to the Clergy and to the Faithful of the Whole Catholic Church on the Role of the Christian Family in the Modern World. November 22, 1981.
- *Catechism of the Catholic Church.* Washington, D.C.: United States Conference of Catholic Bishops, 1997, 2000.
- "Pastoral Constitution on the Church in the Modern World. *Gaudium et Spes.* Promulgated by his Holiness, Pope Paul VI." 7 December 7, 1965.
- Encyclical *Evangelium Vitae* to the Bishops, Priests and Deacons, Men and Women religious, lay Faithful, and all People of Good Will on the Value and Inviolability of Human Life. March 25, 1995.
- John Paul II. *Love and Responsibility.* Revised ed. New York: Farrar, Straus, Giroux, 1981.
- Teresa of Calcutta, Mother. *Love, a Fruit Always in Season: Daily Meditations from the Words of Mother Teresa of Calcutta.* Edited by Dorothy S. Hunt. San Francisco: Ignatius Press, 1987.

FAMILY, THE BODY, AND GOD'S PLAN

- *Catechism of the Catholic Church.* Washington, D.C.: United States Conference of Catholic Bishops, 1997, 2000.
- Lewis, C. S. *The Great Divorce,* New York: Macmillan, 1946.
- John Paul II. *Letter to Families From Pope John Paul II: 1994, Year of the Family.* Boston: Pauline Books and Media, 1994.
- West, Christopher. *The Love That Satisfies: Reflections on Eros & Agape.* West Chester, PA: Ascension, 2007.

Holy Family Prayer

Jesus, Son of God and Son of Mary, bless our family.
Graciously inspire in us the unity, peace, and mutual
love that you found in your own family in the little
town of Nazareth.

Mary, Mother of Jesus and our Mother, nourish our
family with your faith and your love. Keep us close to
your Son, Jesus, in all our sorrows and joys.

Joseph, foster-father to Jesus, guardian and spouse
of Mary, keep our family safe from harm. Help us in
all times of discouragement or anxiety.

Holy Family of Nazareth, make our family one with
you. Help us to be instruments of peace. Grant that
love, strengthened by grace, may prove mightier
than all the weaknesses and trials through which our
families sometimes pass. May we always have God at
the center of our hearts and homes until we are all one
family, happy and at peace in our true home with you.
Amen.

Excerpted from...

Holy Family Prayer Book:
Prayers for Every Family
Missionaries of the Holy Family
ISBN: 978-0-764-822179

To Order, Visit Liguori.org
Call 800-325-9521 • Visit Your Local Bookstore

CPSIA information can be obtained at www.ICGtesting.com
Printed in the USA
LVOW04s1240290815

452037LV00001BB/1/P